The Chaplain in the Field of War

THE CHAPLAIN

IN

THE FIELD OF WAR:

BEING THE

EXPERIENCES OF THE CLERICAL STAFF DURING THE
PRUSSIAN CAMPAIGN OF 1866.

Condensed from the Official Report of the Rev. B. ROGGE,
Chaplain to the Prussian Court.

BY

GEORGE GLADSTONE, F.R.G.S.

LONDON:
BELL & DALDY, YORK STREET, COVENT GARDEN.
1870.

PRINTED BY WILLIAM CLOWES AND SONS, STAMFORD STREET
AND CHARING CROSS.

PREFACE.

THE following pages were prepared for the press before the outbreak of the war between France and Germany, which has already devastated many of the fairest lands of the Continent, and carried mourning and lamentation into many hundreds—nay, even thousands of families. The original intention of the Author was to have made a simple translation of the work, published in Berlin, by the Rev. B. Rogge, under the title of "Die Evangelischen Geistlichen im Feldzuge von 1866," which he prepared, at the request of the Chaplain-General of the Forces, from the official reports sent in to the Prussian Government at the close of that war. It contained, however, an amount of detail which would scarcely have been of interest to English readers, and the result is that the work appears in an abbreviated and somewhat altered form, though still substantially that of the Rev. B. Rogge.

The facts are therefore officially vouched, and the whole tone of the original writer has been so strictly adhered to in the translation, that the Author feels no hesitation in availing himself of some extracts from a letter of Chaplain-General Thiele, to a brother clergyman in the English army, the Rev. Francis Cannon, who has kindly placed the letter at his service. He says: "This work is written with " much warmth and spirit, with a truly Protestant " tone; and is well adapted not only to inform the " readers as to the Christian arrangements in the " army, but also to give them an insight into the life " and feeling of the soldiery, and to convince them " that faith and piety was, by the grace of God, " awake in them, and really contributed to these " grand successes. Several distinguished individuals " who were at the seat of war have testified, from " their personal experience, how truly and con- " scientiously the field chaplains performed their " duty, and have expressed to me their pleasure in " bearing such testimony. I anticipate, therefore, " that the account of the labours of these chaplains " will be all the more interesting to you. In several " quarters the wish has been expressed that this " work should be translated into English; and I " presume that not a few of your countrymen, " especially officers, who take a lively interest in

" the building up of the kingdom of God within the
" army, would rejoice at seeing it appear. I cannot
·" but approve of this view, and hope that the
" spreading of this work amongst the soldiers of
" your country will not remain without a blessing."

The Rev. Francis Cannon, whose encouragement
the Author desires gratefully to acknowledge, fully
endorses the opinion of the work thus expressed by
the Prussian Chaplain-General, and had time permitted would have added some words of his own, in
order to commend the volume to the attention of
those more particularly connected with the British
army.

Under present circumstances, however, it has
appeared desirable not to postpone, even for a
single day, the issue of the work to the public,
believing that it will not only prove a useful com-
panion to, and afford a deeper insight into, the
reports of passing events which are daily presented
by the periodical press, but that it may also serve a
most important purpose in stirring up the public to
still greater efforts than have yet been made for the
relief of the sufferers in the present fearful war.

Some of the scenes on the field of slaughter and
in the hospitals, which are presented in the following
pages, are sad enough; but they will sink almost
into insignificance in comparison with what now

exists in almost every town and village between
Wissembourg and Metz. Were peace to be made
between the belligerents to-morrow, the ministry of
mercy to the sick and wounded must be continued;
and how much may be needed by the tens of
thousands of such sufferers, both in the shape of
bodily care and spiritual consolation, may, the
Author fervently hopes, be better appreciated by
a perusal of this volume.

CLAPHAM COMMON,
August, 1870.

CONTENTS.

CONTENTS.

THE CHAPLAIN IN THE FIELD OF WAR.

CHAPTER I.

THE ORGANIZATION.

THE brief but decisive war of which Germany was
the theatre in the year 1866, was one which, for
many reasons, will in future ages be reckoned
amongst those which have left their mark upon the
world. The shortness of its duration, and the fact
of its being essentially German—for the alliance
between Prussia and Italy caused practically a mere
episode—are probably the principal reasons why we
Englishmen have paid less attention to the details,
and have taken less interest in the results of this
important struggle, than many of our continental
neighbours.

B

Perhaps it is best known as the first great occasion when the superiority of breech-loaders over the old muzzle-loaders was fairly put to the test; and the advantage of the new system was so thoroughly proved, that every nation in Europe which has any pretence to be a military power has since considered it to be one of its first duties to convert its old armoury to the new system, whether by adopting the Prussian needle-gun, or any other application of the breech-loading system which modern science has been able to suggest.   Our opinion is that several of the forms adopted recently by the principal Governments of Europe possess considerable advantages over the needle-gun, which has the merit of creating such a revolution in military affairs; and, though the ratepayers throughout Europe may grumble at the immense cost of the conversion of hundreds of thousands of rifles, it is fairly open to argument whether the increase in the efficiency and the precision of our new weapons of war may not tend in the long-run to the prevention of bloodshed, by rendering nations more unwilling to go to war with one another, and, when such a catastrophe does unhappily take place, by rendering the struggle very much shorter than it would have been under other circumstances.

Our object, however, is not to treat the matter from a purely military point of view—which has already been done most ably by the special correspondents of the leading journals of the day—but, having had the opportunity of reading the official reports of the Protestant army chaplains in the Prussian service, which were sent in to the Chaplain. General of the Forces at the close of the war, we propose to limit our view to that phase of the campaign which they alone can adequately describe. The benefits wrought, and the shortcomings acknowledged by the clergymen who had the charge of the spiritual interests of the army during this trying period, may teach some useful lessons on the one hand, or impart encouragement on the other, to those who have the same duties to discharge towards our own soldiery.

Before accompanying the chaplains to the field, it

will be necessary, however, to enter with some detail into the position which they occupy in the Prussian army, and the arrangements which the Government makes for their comfort and efficiency during active service.

First of all, then, it must be borne in mind that Prussia, and the minor States of Northern Germany which were in alliance with her, are partly Protestant, and partly Roman Catholic, some districts being almost exclusively of one faith, and some equally so of the other. The Government, with true impartiality, maintains a double staff of clergy, so that the men of both confessions shall be equally provided with spiritual consolation. It is with the Protestant chaplains only that we intend to deal, except incidentally—for the ministers of the two faiths were on the best of terms with one another; and we shall have occasionally to describe scenes of interest in which each contributed his part, sinking all minor differences in their desire to do the greatest amount of good under the exceptional circumstances by which they were surrounded.

During this short campaign—commonly called in Germany the six weeks' war, as that brief period was all that elapsed between the commencement of actual hostilities and the conclusion of peace on the 22nd of July—there were on the staff of the Prussian mobile army forty-three Protestant military chaplains, assisted by no less than sixty-four ministers and candidates for the church, who voluntarily undertook regular duty for the time, either in the field or in the hospital, in addition to a large number of lay assistants. It must not be supposed, however, that their labours ended with the making of peace between the two Powers. The following narrative will show that the time of the return march was attended with a much greater amount of suffering, and with far more loss of life, than civilians are apt to imagine; and vast numbers of the invalids had to be left behind in hospital until sufficiently recovered to return home, during which time they were faithfully tended by those volunteers, both clerical and lay, of whom we have just made mention. Large as these numbers may appear to be, the Prussian

Government has acknowledged that there is still
room for improvement; and it is under consideration
whether the number of chaplains should not be
permanently increased, and whether also those who
volunteer in these times of emergency cannot receive
temporarily some official status and better-defined
duties, so as to render their assistance more efficient,
and at the same time relieve them from various
personal inconveniences.

First in rank stands the Chaplain-General of the
Forces. His head-quarters during time of peace are,
of course, at the capital; but during war he is supposed to accompany the army. This, however, was
found to be utterly impracticable, as his duties were
immensely increased when the order for mobilisation
went forth; and his Majesty at once ordered that he
should remain at Berlin. His first business was to
rearrange temporarily the entire clerical staff, so as
to give to that portion of the army which was sent
into the field, as many clergymen as could possibly be
spared from garrison duty, commissioning one of the
regular divisional chaplains in each corps d'armée

as the superior for the time being. From time to time during the progress of the war these appointments had to be modified, as the need of assistance became more pressing now in this, and now in that quarter.

In Prussia they do not have regimental chaplains, as is the case in many other countries, because this would necessitate a very great increase in their number, and would lead to inconvenience, on account of the mixture of creeds among the men. The sphere of operation is, therefore, extended, and the chaplains are placed upon the staff of the division, an arrangement which at the same time renders them more independent of the colonels of the regiments, and gives them a greater authority and influence both over the officers and men. The Austrians adopt the other system; and one of their priests, in the course of conversation with a Prussian military chaplain, attributed the little respect which was paid to them by the Austrian army to their position as mere regimental officers, in consequence of which those colonels who were not seriously disposed held them in contempt, and the men under them naturally followed the example of their superior.

The volunteers must not be passed over without notice. Though forming no part of the organization, and only quasi-officially recognized, they discharged a labour of love which is beyond all praise. · We have already mentioned that sixty-four such persons, in addition to lay assistants, were moved to go to the assistance of their fellow-countrymen who were risking their lives in the camp and on the field of battle. They were usually sent forth at the expense of individual churches or associations for specific purposes; and though supplied with certain necessaries by the Government, they had little other connection with it than what they willingly undertook in the spirit of patriotism. The army had, indeed, scarcely entered into the enemy's country, before it was discovered how inadequate was the clerical staff to the exigencies of the occasion; and within the first fortnight of the campaign several of the churches in West Pomerania devoted a portion of their reserved funds to the laudable object of sending forth spiritual assistance. On hearing of this, the King was so well pleased, that he directed a proclamation to be issued on the 18th of June, in which he thanked these churches for what they had done, and urged all others which had surplus funds in their treasuries to follow the good example set by the Pomeranians. The consequence of this was that 35,635 thalers were sent in to the Minister for Spiritual Affairs from the various churches of Prussia; a considerable portion of which still remains in hand, as a reserve fund for some future occasion, many of the volunteers having been supported by their own congregations, in addition to what was paid into the hands of the Government. Berlin, however, was not to be outdone by Pomerania. A large meeting was held on the 21st June, called by the court preacher, Von Hengstenberg, who, during the previous Schleswig war, had interested himself in a similar manner; and he organized a committee in the capital, for the purpose of making better spiritual provision for their relatives who were then risking their lives in face of the enemy. The result of his eloquent appeal, in-

cluding some contributions from the province of
Brandenburg, was 7,576 thalers, with which they
equipped thirty-five ministers and four assistants, in
addition to supplying a quantity of Bibles and Testaments, and paying for other assistance at several of
the hospitals. The sudden conclusion of the war
left them with a balance in hand of 2,612 thalers,
which still remain as a reserve fund. In Potsdam
also, special collections were made; and Dr. Erdmann, the General Superintendent of the Province of
Silesia, issued an earnest appeal to the congregations
under his charge, who contributed 2,861 thalers, the
whole of which was expended in sending out clergymen from that province, and in supplying them
with a rich store of Testaments, hymn and devotional
books.

While speaking, however, of the voluntary contributions of the different provinces of the kingdom,
we must not omit that one which always stands pre-
eminent in labours of love and mercy, the province
of Westphalia. Not only did the subscriptions pour
in abundantly from all parts of the province, and

from the town of Elberfeld in particular, so that a balance of 2,500 thalers still remains in hand, but numbers of persons offered themselves for the work, both as ministers and laymen, whether in the field or hospital. Of the labours of some of these we shall presently have to make special mention. Nor did they consider only the spiritual wants of the soldiery; they did not forget to supply their temporal necessities, and to furnish many of those little comforts which are so inexpressibly precious to the sick and suffering, especially when away from their own homes. After the war was over, many a soldier presented himself at the society's rooms at Elberfeld, to thank the good people of that town for the invaluable services they had rendered, and for the spiritual comfort of which they had been the dispensers.

Notwithstanding the readiness with which the whole nation responded to the appeals for such assistance, it has become a serious question for the Government, whether, in the event of future wars, it is either prudent or right to allow the spiritual charge of the army in these crises to be in so large a degree dependent upon the interest or enthusiasm of the public, especially as such voluntary assistance cannot be procured by anticipation; and if future wars are to be short (as we hope they may), the emergency will probably have to a great extent passed away ere the succour comes to hand. After the close of the war, the regular chaplains who had been with the several corps d'armée in the field were asked to give their opinions upon this point in their reports to the Chaplain-General of the Forces; and, as may be expected, opinions differed rather widely as to what should be done for the future. Some recommended, as a minimum, one chaplain for every regiment, which would give about two hundred and fifty field preachers to the Prussian army when in a state of mobilisation. Allowing an equal number of Roman Catholic priests, for those who belong to that faith, there would then be a spiritual army of five hundred men in the field, irrespective of their attendants, a number which would form a great burthen to an army on the march. It would, moreover, be a matter of extreme difficulty to find such a number of suitable men in addition to those who would have to remain behind for garrison and depôt duty, as well as to attend the great military hospitals which at such seasons would call for a very large staff. The more general opinion seemed to be in favour of raising the strength of the Protestant chaplains to about the double of what it has hitherto been, say to eight ministers for each corps, and that the organization should be somewhat as follows:—

A superior chaplain to the staff of each general in command;

A chaplain for each of the four infantry brigades;

One for the cavalry division;

One for the reserve artillery;

And one for the large field hospitals;

Making eight in all. The entire army being divided into twelve corps, this would make a total of ninety-six Protestant chaplains; and as the present peace staff consists of forty-eight, it would require a like number to be provided ready to be called out immediately on the issue of the order for mobilisation.

These would then take rank with the regular army chaplains, and be similarly equipped by the Government; the total extra cost of which is estimated at only 50,000 thalers, should their services be un-happily required for a whole twelvemonth. The matter of equipment is one of considerable import-ance, as will be seen presently, when we enter into the details of a clergyman's outfit; the difference in this respect between the regular chaplain and the volunteer, and the want of official status in the case of the latter, having often during the late war thrown them into an unpleasant and false position.

Notwithstanding every provision that can be made beforehand, there will always remain plenty of op-portunities during a time of war for the exercise of the Christian graces, and for the consecration both of one's time and means to the ministry of love to the bodies and souls of the men. What demands there may be upon the hospitals can never be fore-seen, especially as an army in the field suffers much more 'from fever, dysentery, and cholera, than from the hand of the enemy. The graveyards of Moravia, where no fighting took place, tell a much sadder story than those of Bohemia, where the most decisive battles were fought.   The great hospitals in such places as these will afford ample scope for any amount of voluntary agency, should such a scheme for the increase of the official staff as that above described be carried out.

CHAPTER II.

THE OUTFIT.

THE outfit of a military chaplain in time of war will appear to comprise a great many more articles than civilians may be disposed to consider necessary; but experience has proved that upon the whole few, if any, with which they are supplied could well be dispensed with, though some might perhaps be modified to advantage. He is provided by the Government with a carriage, two carriage horses, and one saddle horse, and a couple of soldiers of the train to look after them: a larger supply of conveniences in this respect than even the superior officers of the corps. The carriage has, however, to serve a variety of duties, and the riding horse is quite indispensable for the sake of locomotion. Those who, from want of being good equestrians, or from any other cause, neglected the use of the latter, were frequently put to very great inconvenience thereby, and sometimes ran the risk of being left in the rear just when their services were most needed. It is, moreover, desirable that the chaplain should be in a position to arrive at the rendezvous at the same time as the rest of the staff, which is only possible when he adopts the same means of locomotion as the other officers. Instances did occur during this short war which sufficiently proved the undesirableness of depending too much upon their carriages; indeed, it was absolutely necessary when a battle was imminent that the chaplain should accompany the troops on horseback. The moral effect of his doing so was of itself of some importance, even independently of the desirability of his being at hand when the action commenced.

The chaplain of the first division of Foot Guards, though thoroughly experienced in the duties of his calling, and full of zeal, narrowly escaped being left

c

behind on one occasion ; and his record may serve **as**
an illustration of how necessary it is, even **at the**
cost of considerable self-denial, to be first and fore-
most in times of emergency.   He says in his report,
that on the 27th of June the division to which he
was attached started from Wernersdorf at four o'clock
in the morning, for a village one mile from Braunau.
He had passed a sleepless night, as he was suffering
from a severe toothache; and, expecting that the
day's march would occupy from eight to ten hours,
he decided upon taking his carriage for a part of the
way, and then pushing forwards on horseback to
join the troops at the first rendezvous.   His carriage
had necessarily to take its rank with all the other
vehicles of the train; and the first two miles were
attended by those frequent stoppages which are the
inevitable accompaniment of a long line of vehicles
of the heterogeneous description incident to a baggage train.   At this point, however, he was sum-
marily turned out of the road into a meadow, **to**
wait there until all the troops of the division had
marched past.   Obedience to orders admitted of **no**

alternative. The thought of sitting still in his carriage, perhaps for hours, in the midst of the field, drove away all the effects of the toothache and the weariness resulting from broken rest; so he determined at once to leave the carriage there, and, mounting his horse, he rode forward with the troops. It was a providential thing that he did so. The battle of Trautenau commenced very unexpectedly, before a part of their columns and his carriage had arrived; and as the enemy reoccupied the place after the engagement, the rearward portion of their division had to fall back a considerable distance in order to avoid a conflict. It was three days before he recovered his impedimenta which he left behind in the meadow, during which time his division had fought two important battles. Had he remained behind, he would have been missing at two engagements which urgently demanded his presence, and where he found more than enough to do, both at the places where the sufferers had their wounds dressed, and at the graves of the fallen. His Roman Catholic colleague unfortunately remained in his carriage on that occasion, and was consequently cut off from him during the battles of Burgersdorf and Soor, in addition to which he very nearly fell into the hands of the Austrians, while endeavouring to make his way to the front alone.

The carriage of the chaplain, however, has its uses, and they are not a few; and the indulgence of a carriage is justified in a military point of view by the fact that the resting days of the army are just those of greatest activity for the minister, as he must avail himself of them for his spiritual duties, whatever the day of the week may be. On these occasions he has perhaps to drive to three or four different places, for the purpose of holding public worship with the several brigades of his corps, and these are sometimes encamped at considerable distances from one another. While thus driving about the carriage forms his study, and furnishes almost the only opportunity of quiet reading and gathering up his thoughts preparatory to the service he is about to conduct. It also carries all the articles required for public worship, which, in the opinion of

a Lutheran, are quite indispensable. The outfit
supplied by the Prussian Government will naturally
appear to us to be unnecessarily large, and some of
the chaplains suggest that it might be reduced with
advantage. It consisted of a complete set of communion plate, an altar cloth, a crucifix, and two
candlesticks. The crucifixes were made of cast iron,
and were much too heavy, the candlesticks, made
of the same material, were practically useless, because at an open-air service the lights would rarely
burn, and they are to be found in every church in
Germany, whether Roman Catholic or Protestant.
Of course the chaplain must take, in addition to his
personal baggage, a Bible, church-service, and hymn-
book for his own use, in addition to a supply of
these and other useful reading for distribution to
the sick and wounded. The soldiers in hospital were
always most thankful for any books which would
serve to relieve them of their tedium; and the
chaplains had constant cause to regret that their
stock was necessarily so limited. They should
never be without a supply of letter-paper and pencils,

as the soldiers rarely have any with them, and when laid aside by disease or wounds they naturally desire to inform their relatives at home of what has befallen them, and subsequently of their recovery, if indeed such is happily the case. Very often, too, the chaplain not only had to supply the writing materials, but also act the part of amanuensis. We shall come presently to instances when these duties had to be performed—duties which, it may readily be inferred, were generally of a painful character, as they were of course only called for in cases of extreme illness.

Having thus shown, in some detail, how necessary the carriage and horses are to the military chaplain, it is almost refreshing to an Englishman, who is so constantly reminded by the ever active newspaper correspondents of all the little defects in our organisation, to find that even Prussia is not quite perfect. The horses are spoken of as having been supplied just in the condition in which they came from the hands of Mother Nature, and the shoes upon their feet were in a very bad condition : the harness and the carriages were also supplied by the same department, and needed more attention than they received; the consequence of which was that breakdowns sometimes occurred, which not only delayed the occupant, but caused a block which stopped the whole of the baggage train in the rear until it could be got out of the way. The carriages, moreover, were suitable enough for the level plain which is so characteristic of Central Prussia; but the officials had entirely forgotten that the frontier lands of the Austrian empire are everywhere mountainous, and as soon as they reached this part the chaplains had to get breaks put on the wheels as best they could. Moreover, the two soldiers of the train who, as already mentioned, are told off for the service of the chaplain, and whose special duties are to look after his equipage, are not selected by him; in consequence of which very unsuitable men were sometimes allotted to them, who gave the ministers much trouble and annoyance, and seriously impaired their usefulness. The remedy for this is, however, pretty much in the hands of the chaplains themselves. Be taking a little trouble before the campaign begins, they can generally pick out a couple of respectable, well-conducted men; and a suggestion to the superior officer in whose hands the appointment rests, that he would like to have such and such an one, would scarcely ever remain unheeded.

There is a third person, however, who holds an important office under the chaplain, and of whom we shall hear more anon—the sexton. He indeed combines several offices in one person, and the military regulations require that he shall be a subaltern of experience. He has to see that the two soldiers do their duty, keeping the carriage and horses in proper order and in constant readiness; to act as clerk in the public services, and to make all the necessary arrangements for them, which, when held in the open air, involved a good deal of trouble and forethought. Some of the chaplains in the late war complained that the sextons were rather a trouble to them than otherwise; but this could only have arisen from the men having been unsuited for or unacquainted with the duties of the post. It is strongly recommended that, whenever possible, the divisional sexton who is attached to the military chaplain in garrison duty during the time of peace should attend him also when in the field, as he knows the habits of his pastor, and is also, to some extent, personally known to the troops. That he should be a man of such experience is, however, all the more necessary when the chaplain over him is an extra one appointed only for the period of mobilisation, and who has yet to learn the distinctions between the different battalions and companies under his charge. The sexton has no official rank as such, and no distinctive uniform. During the late campaign several inconveniences were found to result from the want of these ; and it has been suggested that, in future, they should rank as sergeant-majors, and that under certain circumstances they might even carry arms. For want of being officially recognised, quarters were rarely provided for them in some of the divisions; and they had sometimes to endure needless hardships in consequence, besides being delayed in the discharge of their duties. The only distinctive badge which they were authorised to wear (and which, moreover, some of them never received, and others only towards the end of the campaign) was a white band with a red cross upon it. Practically, however, this formed no distinction at all, for most of the loiterers in the train of the army, who followed it out of mere curiosity, adopted for their own protection this badge, intended to indicate exclusively those engaged in deeds of mercy.

The dress of the military chaplains had undergone considerable alterations since the Schleswig war, which were generally accepted as great improvements; but the silk scarf round the neck, which had been prescribed, was quickly abandoned as unsuitable for a campaign, and a violet-coloured band of silk with broad white stripes upon it was worn round the arm instead, as a distinctive badge of the Protestants. Mr. Rogge, one of the court chaplains, mentions, that when his Roman Catholic colleague saw the scarf, he prophesied that he would be shot dead in the first fight, for a badge that was so pro-

minent would be sure to be taken for an important
military sign. He indeed only wore it once, when
he was amongst the officers collected to give the
royal salute to her Majesty the Queen of Prussia, on
leaving the railway station at Brieg, when so many
glances were directed towards him, and so many
remarks were overheard about it, that he admitted
the justice of his Roman Catholic friend's criticism,
and never gave the enemy the opportunity of testing
the correctness of the prophecy. Simple as the
official costume now is, it does not actually fulfil
what is required of it. A black coat with single
front, and a black silk vest of the same make, is now
the regulation in time of war; so far well, but the
length of the coat-tails is a very grave matter. The
rule is that they shall extend two handbreadths below
the knee; now this is a length which is found very
unsuitable for riding on horseback, and more especially so in dirty weather. It will answer all
useful purposes if it just covers the knee; but there
is a more important reason why it should be so
altered. The present regulation length is so nearly

akin to that of Roman Catholic 'priests throughout
Europe, that the wearers are scarcely to be recognised as Protestants; and several of them, during the
course of the war, actually received the customary
kiss on the hand from the Roman Catholic population in Austria and Bohemia, as they could not, in
all cases, avoid receiving this tribute of respect.

Before accompanying the army to the field, we
must say a few words about those ministers who
volunteered their services at this crisis. They did
not come under the field regulations of the regular
chaplains, and were but sorrily provided for by the
Government. They were only supplied with one
horse and a foot soldier, in consequence of which
they jocularly called their official superiors " the
pachas of three horsetails," while, at the same time,
they had good reason to envy the latter their advantages. One horse, with an unmounted soldier,
was in fact of little service. If the minister rode on,
the soldier could not keep up with him, and then on
arriving at his destination he would be without any
one to look after the stabling of his horse, which was

often a matter of considerable trouble, on account of
the crowded state of the quarters. Moreover, it was
not always so easy to arrange a place of meeting, as
the movements of the army were uncertain, and
great confusion often arose from the places over
the frontier having Bohemian as well as German
names, the former being frequently almost unpro-
nounceable. These ministers often found it to be
their safest and wisest plan to employ the horse
merely to carry their baggage, and make their
journeys on foot. This expedient, however, entailed
a considerable loss of time, as well as unnecessary
fatigue. The whole of this part of the service indeed
requires remodelling; and it is a question whether
the pachas of three horsetails should not be confined
exclusively to the mobile army, and that all so
attached should be provided in the manner already
described. Another class of chaplains might then
be specially appointed for the great immovable
hospitals, who would not want any horse at all,
as the means of communication throughout Europe
are now such as to enable any one to reach very

near to his destination without much interruption even in time of war; in which case the military sexton would not be required, but a lay deacon might be substituted with the greatest advantage. The exigencies of the service might perhaps require that some should be available for either duty, and these might be most appropriately supplied with a carriage and two horses, which would afford them certain facilities of locomotion, and be especially useful in making a circuit of the different hospitals.

During the late war the chaplains suffered considerable inconvenience for want of proper maps and plans of the country which they were about to enter; and there does not seem to be any substantial reason why they should not be supplied with the official plans which are prepared for the general staff.

Few of these details or suggestions may be of any practical application to the British army, constituted as it is on so different a model from that of the Prussian; but they will serve to illustrate the personal narratives which occur in the following chapters, and to account for some of the defects which occasionally made themselves patent. Nevertheless, we may say unreservedly that the military chaplains of the Prussian army, and their voluntary assistants, did a great and glorious work during those few weeks of desperate struggle, and that there are many who will have reason to remember with gratitude the season of toil through which at that time they passed.

CHAPTER III.

PUBLIC WORSHIP.

No sooner had the signal to advance been given, than the Prussian army pushed forward with unprecedented vigour to meet the Austrian and allied legions in Southern Germany and Bohemia. The rapidity of the march, which was so destructive to the enemy, was also a great impediment to the military chaplain in the discharge of his pastoral duties.

From the time when the army entered Bohemia, until the day that the war ceased before the gates of Vienna and Presburg, the military columns ever pressed forward with restless haste. The old cry of " Forward !" was the constant watchword of the Prussian army and its leaders. The greater portion of the troops scarcely rested more than three or four days from the 22nd of June to the 22nd July, at which time the peace was concluded. The movements of the Army of the Maine were almost equally constant, and during its advance active engagements with the enemy, of more or less importance, followed one another in rapid succession, almost day by day.

We propose in the present chapter to illustrate from the official reports of the chaplains themselves the character of the public services which they were able to hold during the march.

They were beset with difficulties, and those in particular who were attached to the respective head-quarters, and who therefore had to advance with their respective staffs, were sometimes sorely disposed to think that their office was of very little practical utility. One in the 4th corps d'armée writes, for instance, as follows:—"It was behind "Reichenau, where, after many ineffectual attempts, "I arranged with the commander of a regiment, on "the morning of a day of rest, that the whole

D

" regiment should be assembled at four o'clock in
" the afternoon for public worship and the celebra-
" tion of the Lord's Supper. All was in order, the
" bread and wine having been procured with great
" difficulty, when at noon the command arrived from
" head-quarters for the troops to march forward at
" two o'clock. I can hardly describe my bitter
" disappointment." Yet such was the experience
of nearly all the field preachers during this period.

As a general rule the superior officers in the
Prussian army were favourably disposed to the
chaplains, and ready to render them all the assistance in their power; but, notwithstanding the
facilities given them, they had innumerable difficulties to contend with in the discharge of
their duty. Up to a late hour one evening it
was generally quite uncertain whether the next
was to be a day of rest or not; and in such a
state of doubt the officers were discouraged from
issuing orders for a religious service, not knowing whether it might not have to be withdrawn
immediately afterwards. Sometimes the troops were

very fatigued, and the time that could be spared
for resting could not be curtailed for the purpose
of Divine worship; at other times they had to wash
and mend their clothes, which of course suffer
greatly under the constant wear and tear of a campaign; while the cantonments of the troops were
often much too widely spread over the country to
admit of the men being collected together at a short
notice. It was necessary indeed on some occasions
to adopt the Pauline maxim of preaching " in
season and out of season;" and thus a halt upon
the march was sometimes turned into a service
for God, without interfering with the military
operations.

It will not be doubted that some commanders
rendered much greater facilities in this respect than
others. One general of division repeatedly ordered
public worship to be held at the rendezvous of his
troops after each day's march, an arrangement
which was accompanied with the happiest results.
Of course such services as these must necessarily
be brief, lest they should interfere with the bodily

rest of the soldiers, and a quarter of an hour thus spent, might be more profitable than a longer and more formal service. The usual morning prayers prescribed for the army might in like manner be used before starting upon the day's march; and who can tell what might be the value of a few sentences of God's word to the soldier who is about to go forth in the face of danger and perhaps even of death? A service something of this nature is described by one of the field chaplains in the following terms:—" We arrived in Kamienetz, after " a fatiguing march, late in the afternoon of the " 8th of July, when General von M. announced that " a public thanksgiving to God for the battle which " had been won should be celebrated at the first " rendezvous next morning in the presence of the " whole division. We started between four and five " o'clock in the morning, and I rode forward with " the officers of the staff to the place which had " been appointed for the purpose. The division " halted at the village of Hlinsoo at seven o'clock, " the regiments piled their arms, and each brigade

"formed itself into square. The days which had
"just passed had spoken powerfully to all hearts,
"directing those who had been protected in danger
"to God, whose power had so manifestly been dis-
"played,—and, through the death of thousands who
"succumbed in the bloom of their strength, ad-
"monishing those who were victorious to care for
"the safety of their souls. I dismounted from my
"horse, and at once stepped into the square formed
"by the brigade. We sang some verses of the
"hymn, 'Ach bleib mit deiner Gnade,' accompanied
"by the regimental band, which was followed by
"a short sermon, an extempore prayer, and the
"benediction, concluding with another verse of the
"same hymn. The troops then stepped forward,
"shouldered their arms, and immediately resumed
"their march."

In another division, which fortunately .enjoyed
more leisure than many, it was arranged that, whenever possible, a short service should be held every
evening for about half an hour, either in the open
air or a church, as might be most convenient. These

troops generally came into quarters early in the
afternoon, so that they had time to rest and refresh
themselves before the evening service; but if the
rule were more generally laid down, the opportunities of doing so, without interfering with their
military duties, would be found of more frequent
occurrence than many would be disposed at first
thought to admit. Moreover, if such were the understanding, the officers would make their arrangements accordingly, so that there would be no loss of
time in carrying out the details.

The difficulties which the military chaplain had to
contend with were not limited to the period when
the army was pushing forward with such restless
haste, and fighting new battles almost day by day.
During the negotiations for the settlement of the
terms of peace, even, when a large portion of the
army was in a state of comparative rest, new sources
of inconvenience arose which considerably impeded
them in the discharge of their duties. One of the
most formidable of these was the immense extent of
ground then occupied by the Prussian army. At

that period the Army of the Maine, and the reserve corps, were scattered over most of the southern provinces of the Germanic Confederation; but the inconvenience was felt most by those corps which occupied Bohemia and Moravia. In these countries the troops of a single division were often scattered over an area of more than two hundred square miles, so that the chaplain lost an immense amount of valuable time in the mere act of travelling from one part of his charge to another. Imagine him also in an enemy's country, with the peasantry all speaking a foreign language, seeking out the soldiers even of a single company, and having to hunt over several villages and all the intermediate farmsteads, and you may realise some idea of the labour required in visiting his flock.

We have already mentioned that the customary distinctions between the Sunday and other days of the week could not be maintained during a campaign of this nature; and the usual military rule of enforcing attendance at the appointed services had also in most cases to be abandoned. Indeed it was only at the special thanksgiving services which were held after signal victories, and other occasions of equal importance, that even the portion of the corps which was off duty was officially commanded to be present. With the rest it was a purely voluntary act. The time and place, when and where, the services were to be held were officially announced, but it was left to every man's conscience whether he should attend or not. The readiness with which they at all times responded to the appeal moved the hearts of many of the chaplains; and they felt much encouragement and a deeper call to earnestness in their work, from the feeling that all those who stood before them were there in consequence of a real desire for the blessings of Divine worship. Some of them even felt that it would be a glorious thing if the same freedom could be permitted to the army in time of peace, so that they might feel themselves to be addressing willing hearts, instead of to men compelled to be present by military rules. Another feature which was sufficiently marked as to attract attention was, that when the religious services happened to be held upon the Sunday, there was generally a better attendance than upon other occasions. Notwithstanding the complete disorganization of all social systems by the exigencies of military service in such times, there seemed to be still a feeling of regard for the day, which perhaps was heightened by the remembrance of the trials and dangers which each one had undergone through the week, and by the knowledge that at that time prayer would be ascending to Heaven from all the churches of the land, for God's blessing upon them, and His protection in the hour of danger.

The hearty co-operation of nearly all the superior officers of the army, and the readiness with which large numbers of the men responded to the invitations to public worship, afforded great encouragement to the chaplains, and rendered them much less fastidious than they might otherwise have been in the selection of the places for holding their meetings. They were held indeed under almost every variety of circumstances that can be imagined. Sometimes the scene was a ridge of hills, the summits of which

formed their only shelter; sometimes in the seclusion
of an orchard of fruit trees, or of one of the large
plantations of osiers which are so common in Lower
Austria and Moravia; while, at other times, the
troops would be assembled in the empty market-
place of some Bohemian town, with a statue of the
Virgin Mary or of St. John Nepomuck (the patron
saint of the country) in the centre, reminding them
of Paul's sermon at Athens before the altar of the
unknown God. Not uncommonly the associations
of the place suggested the parable of the sower as
the most appropriate text, the illustrations adopted
by our Lord being all before the preacher's eyes at
the time. Although this war was confined to Central
Europe, we have the record of one public service
which was held upon the water, the chaplain having
embraced the opportunity of preaching to some two
hundred soldiers as he accompanied them on the
15th of July, from Gemünden to Lohr down the
River Maine in two boats which were fastened together. He took his seat on the raised stern of
one of the boats, and invited the soldiers to join him

in singing the hymn, " Ach bleib mit deiner Gnade."
He then read the 91st Psalm, and gave a short
address, to a most attentive audience, impressed
with the beauty and calmness of the spot for worshipping God. The principal operations of the army
being in a country which was essentially Roman
Catholic, nearly all the churches in which services
to the troops were held from time to time belonged
to that communion; and the Protestant chaplains
availed themselves of them equally with the others,
notwithstanding the apparent incongruity of singing
the celebrated Lutheran hymn, " Ein, feste Burg ist
" unser Gott," in a building decorated with pictures
of St. Dominic or of Ignatius Loyola. All kinds of
buildings, even those which were of scarcely re-
putable character, were availed of for such purposes :
circuses, dancing-saloons, taprooms, theatres, wait-
ing-rooms at railway stations, courts of law, council
chambers, barns, and sheds for waggons, were all in
their turn sanctified by the word of God and by
prayer—reminding one of the words of Paul, " All is
" yours."

One chaplain thus describes his own experience of the various makeshifts that fell to his lot during these few weeks, while most of the others could furnish incidents which would seem equally droll at other times and under other circumstances. He says: " In Pardubitz the noisy tumult of drinkers in " an adjoining taproom formed a remarkable con- " trast to our quiet worship. In Kurlena it was " quite dark, and one halfpenny candle supplied all " the light we had. I was often reminded of the " manger in Bethlehem. For instance, in Briesa " and Swestar we stood up to our ankles in mud, and " the rain poured down in such streams that I was " obliged in the communion service to cover the " bread over with the lid of a box whilst conse- " crating it, and with the sleeve of my gown while " dispensing it. At Nedelist the peasantry were " carting manure in front of the door of our barn " during all the service; and at St. Wenzel the " bell tower was used as a stable for the horses " of the hussars, and they poked their noses into " the church and neighed. In Zugmantel a weaver's

" house was converted into a church, and the loom
" served the place of an altar."

The Rev. B. Rogge says: "According to my
" experience, fields, forests, or meadows are always
" to be had for public worship, when at least it
" consisted merely of singing, prayer, and preaching,
" without the addition of the Lord's Supper, and I
" preferred them above all other localities. It is
" good for the soldier to be reminded of his pilgrim
" and wandering life by such external circum-
" stances. References to the patriarchs and the
" Old Testament heroes are much more effectually
" made under God's free heaven than in closed
" rooms, which are often damp, and much too small
" to accommodate the number of hearers that
" may assemble. The very fact of being in the
" open air enables the preacher to present the
" events of sacred history, which for the most part
" took place out of doors, with greater force. The
" application to military life of such subjects as the fol-
" lowing was, moreover, so natural :—Jacob's dream,
" and his acknowledgment, 'Certainly the Lord is

" ' in this place, and I knew it not;' his departure
" from Bethel, and his happy return ; his struggle
" with God at Peniel ; the journeyings of the chil-
" dren of Israel in the desert; the thanksgiving festival
" of Joshua at the Jordan ; the festival of Samuel
" at Mizpeh, and the Ebenezer established there ;
" David's various campaigns, and his deliverances
" out of the hand of the enemy; and a hundred
" other circumstances of sacred history could also be so
" much more easily and graphically explained when
" the similarity of the situation with regard to their
" outdoor life as an army appealed directly to the
" understanding.   I think I shall never preach
" again with such comfort as I did on the Fifth
" Sunday after Trinity from the call to Peter,
" ' Launch out into the deep.'   On this occasion our
" division lay before Königinhof, with the Silesian
" mountains behind us, from which we had just
" emerged after forced marches and victorious
" battles; before us were the heights bordering the
" Elbe, across which was our future route, soon to
" become memorable in history for the series of

" battles of which it would be the scene. The
" impression of that sermon will, I believe, be much
" more permanent in the minds of many of the
" hearers, because they had the wide plain which
" they were about to traverse within range of vision,
" than if their view had been confined within narrow
" walls. Holding the service in the open air ensures
" also this great advantage, that the minister has no
" anxiety about the amount of accommodation, know-
" ing that all who are ordered out of their quarters
" and have assembled together will find room. It is
" grievous and vexatious to secure the attendance of
" a part of the troops, perhaps for the first time,
" and then find that the place selected for Divine
" worship will scarcely furnish room for half the
" number who come to attend the service. When
" this happened to me, I invariably adjourned from
" the church or room into the open air. I had
" arranged a service one Sunday afternoon for a
" battalion of our division ; it was the first Sunday
" we had spent in Lower Austria, and the first day
" of rest we had enjoyed after some very long

" marches. As my quarters were more than four
" miles distant, the appointment had to be made by
" an orderly, and I had no idea of the locality. The
" weather was so uncertain that the village church
" had been announced as the place of meeting; and
" when I arrived, I found hundreds of soldiers,
" not only of the battalion in question, but also of
" others which were cantoned in the neighbourhood,
" gathered together in front of a small dark chapel
" scarcely large enough to hold eighty people. I
" would not disperse the soldiers without first feed-
" ing them with the word of God ; and so, with the
" help of the commander, to whom I still owe thanks
" for prompt and friendly help, a suitable place was
" quickly found, and in less than a quarter of an hour
" everything was prepared for field preaching, with
" the help of the appliances for the altar brought out
" of the carriage. I have almost invariably observed
" that the officers, as well as the soldiers, preferred
" the service being held in the open air, and often
" fancied they displayed greater readiness to assemble
" together under the canopy of heaven."

All the chaplains felt inspirited at seeing such handsome, powerful troops, bearing the evidences of hard labour on their sunburnt faces, forming themselves into square in close rows, with their officers standing in front of each side, leaning upon their swords, while the superior officers with their staff surrounded the altar, which was erected in the midst, and decked with its beautiful red cloth and iron cross. At the large gatherings on special occasions the standards also waved in front of each battalion. All was order, purpose, and significance, notwithstanding the apparent want of external forms. One farmer, in whose field a service was held, was so struck with the scene, that he announced his determination to erect a memorial stone on the spot where the altar stood.

E

CHAPTER IV.

PREACHING IN ROMAN CATHOLIC CHURCHES.

As soon as the ¦Prussian army had passed the
frontiers, the 'troops entered countries which are
more or less ¸exclusively Roman Catholic, and in
bad weather the chaplains were instructed to make
use of the churches belonging to that denomination.
This inevitably entailed sundry difficulties, not
merely from those who naturally claimed the
spiritual authority in the place, but also because
the commanders of different divisions of the army
held diverse views upon the subject. Some had not
the least compunction in taking their stand upon
the military rule of might, while others felt conscientious scruples upon the point, and would not

avail themselves of the power which was actually in their own hands, lest any suspicion should be aroused that the war was one of religion. Indeed, the greatest circumspection was necessary, in order to guard against the almost incredible charges which were raked up by the Ultramontanes before the war began for the purpose of exciting religious fanaticism, and of stamping it with such a character.

Under the exigencies of the case, it might, however, be regarded as an excess of caution to renounce altogether the use of the Roman Catholic churches in places where no other suitable accommodation existed, when the weather would not admit of open-air services. The consciences of the Romish clergy could not be violated by their use, as the request of the army of occupation carries all the force of law, and the priests could always protect themselves by a simple protest. Moreover, if they were much troubled at such a visitation, the church could easily have been purified from any spiritual miasma that might have been left behind by a fresh act of consecration. Nor could the holding of a

Protestant service have been regarded by any one as
so much more improper than the using of the
consecrated edifice as a barrack for the quartering
of prisoners, or for any other secular purpose; yet
no one hesitated in thus availing of them.

Many interesting stories are told by the different
chaplains as to the effect of these services upon the
priests, and the people in their cure. The general
result was to promote a spirit of harmony and good-
will between them. It was their duty as well as
their desire not to offend needlessly those whose
churches they were occupying, and to show in how
much they agreed, rather than where they differed.
Thus they frequently became good friends, and much
of the religious animosity which had been stirred up
and fostered prior to the breaking out of the war, by
misrepresentations of the doctrines taught, and as to
the godlessness of the Prussian soldiery, was allayed
when they came into actual contact. The Austrian
clergy, indeed, frequently expressed their astonish-
ment at the religious feeling exhibited by the Prussian troops, confessing at the same time that in the

imperial army there was never the same readiness to join in public worship. One of the chaplains reports that a Roman Catholic deacon said to him at the close of one of the Protestant communion services which was held in his church, " The fact is, " God has given you the victory because your " soldiers fear Him. It is not so with ours."

The Bishop of Linz, at the meeting of the Lower Austrian session, made the following remark: "It " has been asserted that Austria is the refuge of the " Jesuits: the victorious army had forty-one Jesuits " in its midst; our army had not one. The Prussian " army was their refuge ; the Austrian army unfor- " tunately was not." It is not clear what he meant to imply by this, for there seems to be no evidence that the Romanist chaplains in the Prussian army belonged to that society; and the Rev. B. Rogge distinctly asserts that his colleague was not one of them, his testimony being the result of a close intimacy of three months. Perhaps he rather wished to imply that it was the doctrine of Jesus, and the religious principles and fear of God which was in

the hearts of the Prussians, which wrought the victory ; in opposition to the Concordat, which up to
this period had been held in such esteem by his
compatriots, but which recent events have happily
brought into disfavour.

To show how little some of the priests in the rural
districts of Bohemia understood about Protestantism,
we quote the following from one of the chaplains'
reports : " The curate at P—— asked me whether
" we had sacred pictures ; and he was quite astonished
" when I described to him how our churches were
" arranged.   Up to this time he had been acquainted
" only with the strictly reformed church.   When I
" gave him the service-book, he found to his surprise
" that everything written therein was contained in
" the missal ; and he was in raptures of delight to
" think that we both stood upon the common foun-
" dation of the ancient church."

One Roman Catholic priest in Lower Austria,
whose church had frequently been used during the
time of the armistice, asked permission, when peace
was declared, to say a few words to the soldiers :—it

was to express his joy at the pious feelings he had
observed amongst them, and at the Christianlike
behaviour they had exhibited during their sojourn
in his district, and to wish them the blessing of God
on their return home.   Others, who had not the
courage to state it as openly as he did, were also
effectively cured of many prejudices against the
Protestants.

The Roman Catholic population generally crowded
to their services, always behaving with great propriety; and they listened attentively, even when
they did not understand German, the language of
the country being spoken exclusively in the retired
and mountainous parts of Bohemia.   The dispensing
of both elements in the Lord's Supper made an
evident impression, and the people betrayed a kind
of envious surprise as they watched the passing round
of the chalice.   Perhaps the remembrance of the time
when their Hussite forefathers celebrated the Lord's
Supper after the same manner was reawakened
in many hearts.   The chalice is still to be seen
in the decorations of many churches in Bohemia—

mute witnesses of that reformation which at one
time stirred this people so mightily.

The population generally showed no hostile
feeling against the Protestant chaplains—not even
ill-will against them as invaders of their sanctuaries;
but many, on the contrary, have been heard to avow
a great regard for the Protestant worship; and they
also gratified their natural love for music by joining
in the singing of the hymns, which evidently afforded
them real pleasure. Sometimes, indeed, Romanists
were met with whose countenances indicated a
fanatical hatred against the heretics, as they would
call them; and who, during the Protestant service,
would be seen at a side chapel, before a picture of
the Virgin, or some saint, going through their
prayers, and telling their rosary with the greatest
diligence, in order to counteract the influence of the
evil spirits gathered in their church. But these
were rare exceptions; and often countenances that
exhibited the greatest dejection at the beginning of
the services would clear up more and more as they
went on, and the remark would afterwards be made

that, after all, the dreaded profanation of the house
of God was not so bad as they had anticipated. The
Rev. B. Rogge says, in one of his reports: "An old
" postmaster, who dwelt in a place where I used the
" church for public worship on several successive
" days, showed greater attention on each occasion,
" and also remained during the celebration of the
" Lord's Supper. One day he waited for me at the
" church-door, to put this question, 'Wherein lies
" ' the real difference between us and you?' I
" sought to place before him with all brevity the
" principal doctrinal differences between the one and
" the other; and when I spoke of the Pope, in con-
" clusion, he said, with manifest indignation, 'Ah, we
" ' ought to have got rid of him long ago. He never
" ' did us any good.'"

"The priests themselves did not, as a rule, regard
" the profanation of their churches as a matter of
" very serious consequence; but there is no doubt
" that they did fear their influence might be weakened
" by our preaching; and, as honest and conscientious
" men, who can blame them? They did not mind

" our worshipping in their churches, so long as they
" could keep their own flock from taking part in
" our services.   It was impossible to be displeased
" with them, for it was quite evident that they knew
" it only wanted a spark and a bit of tinder to set
" the old land of the Hussites in a blaze again.   The
" people, indeed, often debated these questions
" openly with their clergy; and had the Prussian
" army remained much longer in Moravia or Bo-
" hemia, the Protestant church would certainly have
" taken root in the land, without any real attempt
" on the part of the military chaplains at propa-
" gandism."   Not unfrequently they were even
present at the services, not as secret attendants or
inquisitive spectators, but showing evident pleasure
and sincere joy in everything that illustrated the
common foundation of Christian faith.   They sometimes lent a helping hand in the necessary preparations, inquired after the wishes of the chaplains, and
gave the necessary instructions to the sacristans.
Field Chaplain G—— mentions one who, at the
close of the service, thanked him for the sermon in

warm and hearty words, assuring him that the only difference between their respective views was in externals, and that both would equally be saved through Christ. Another reports that, "In Z—— "the three Roman Catholic clergymen were present "at my communion service, and one of them did "not hesitate to lead me to the altar and the pulpit "in his ecclesiastical robes." A third says: "Many "Roman Catholic priests met me so far as to provide "the communion wine, and begged me to use their "vasa sacra. They also generally attended public "worship with the people, especially in Hungary. "The priest at R—— saluted me with these words: "'Though we may be enemies in name, we are "'nevertheless brothers in Jesus Christ.'"

Divisional Chaplain Steinwender, of the 1st corps d'armée, relates that it never occurred to him to ask for the use of a Roman Catholic church, until one day a priest offered his church of his own accord. From that time forward he never hesitated to make use of other churches, and he even went to the Archbishop of Olmutz, at Kremsier, to ask permission to

conduct military service in one of his. The Archbishop cleared his throat twice, and then said, " Well,
" yes, if it must be so ; but otherwise I cannot give
" my permission, as you in your present position
" know very well." Ultimately he did not grant the
use of the parish church, but allowed the service to
take place in one belonging to the Piarist monks.
He subsequently issued a pastoral letter to his
subordinates, requesting them to place their churches
at the disposal of the Prussian army chaplains. It
may be that many of them were actuated by the
feeling that it was best policy to put a good face on
a bad business, instead of creating vexatious conflicts
by refusals which would have proved fruitless, as
they must ultimately have come off worst; but
many were certainly actuated by the principle of
brotherly love, as they exceeded what was necessary,
and carried out the apostolic injunction, " Use hospi-
" tality one to another without grudging," opening
their houses freely to them in a manner which might
be imitated to advantage by the Protestant ministers
of Prussia.

The chaplains always acknowledged the kindness received at the hands of their Roman Catholic brethren by avoiding, as far as possible, any interference with their stated services, as well as with their prejudices. One case, however, is on record where the two services were carried on simultaneously; but this happened quite unwittingly; and, as the sequel shows, it created a bond of friendship rather than a scandal. We will let the chaplain tell the story in his own words. " It was arranged " by the sergeant that the use of the church should " be granted for the service appointed to be held on " the following day. At seven o'clock in the " morning the company mustered in front of the " church; the latter was open and empty, in expec- " tation, as I imagined, of our coming, so we accord- " ingly entered. I took my stand before the rail " enclosing the space round the altar, and began the " service. The townspeople present I took to be " inquisitive spectators. During the singing the " priest belonging to the place made his appearance, " went into the sacristy, came out again by a side

" door behind my back, and stepped in front of the
" altar. He held mass, the bell rang, the pyx was
" exhibited, and the people fell down upon their
" knees, whilst I preached from the words, 'Be a
" ' good soldier of Jesus Christ.' Had I known the
" actual circumstances of the case, I might have
" stopped; but I supposed that the priest considered
" the two services might be advantageously united,
" and I preached on. After the service the whole
" mystery was cleared up. No request had been
" communicated to the priest for the setting apart of
" the church for our service. The lieutenant of the
" company, whose duty it had been to send the
" order, had been sitting on live coals all the time,
" wondering what would happen at the close. He
" came forward at once, looking very much discon-
" certed, and accused himself as the sole author of
" the disturbance. The worthy priest consoled him
" with these words: 'We have each served God in
" ' our own way.' Combined churches are not un-
" common, but I think this combined service will not
" easily be matched."

No sooner, however, had the armistice been concluded, than the clergy showed a general disposition to refuse the accommodation which they had so readily granted during the prosecution of the war, and on the return march decided refusals were not uncommon. One dean replied: " I see you are " Protestant, therefore it is impossible for me to " oblige you;" and though urged by the example of others, as well as by argument, he was so persistent that the officer broke off the negotiation with these words: " Our Lord God will lend us His heaven and " His earth for our preaching, and will bless us " without your church." In passing through the town of B—— the commander of the troops applied to the magistrate, who placed the church of the Minorites at his disposal. In the evening, however, a messenger waited upon the chaplain to inform him that the church could not be had, handing him a letter, which ran as follows:—

" HONOURABLE MILITARY COMMANDER,

" The undersigned has received information " which is disagreeable both to him and his people.

" He hears that a Protestant service will be held in
" his cloister church at ten o'clock to-morrow morning,
" for the military who are quartered in his district.
" As this is not compatible with his views and con-
" victions, and the armistice exists at the present
" time, he considers it necessary hereby to declare
" that he is opposed to the holding of the said service
" in his church.

    " Minorite Convent, B——, 24th August, 1866.
                " FATHER PHILIP M——, Guardian."

The chaplain proceeds to report that: " Next
" morning the General in command sent me a
" written order to hold the service at the appointed
" time in the said church. I went in some trepida-
" tion, as, after the guardian's letter, I expected to
" meet an enraged populace, worked up to a state of
" fanaticism by the monks, as the defenders of their
" church, added to which a captain had told me
" that the inhabitants of B—— were disposed to
" resist in every way. I was prepared for stones and
" even a street fight—for the service had to be held
' under all circumstances, because, had the resist-

" ance been successful, all the Roman Catholic
" churches would have been closed to us in future.
" To my surprise, I found a quiet little town with
" friendly inhabitants. The magistrate had settled
" the matter, and the church was opened to us at the
" appointed time. I remained more than an hour
" with the guardian, who combined a holy simplicity
" with monkish shrewdness. His trouble had been
" lest the inhabitants of the place should hear the
" Protestant service. The doors towards the street
" stood open, and the people streamed in numbers
" into the church; but the only entrances to the
" organ-loft and chancel were through the cloister,
" and these he kept well guarded; the monks being
" greatly offended at their superior because he pre-
" vented them by all kinds of subterfuges from
" hearing the sermon. I stood quietly while the
" good man made his excuses to me, saying that the
" inhabitants of the place were too presumptuous,
" that they troubled the holy peace of the cloister,
" and destroyed all piety. During my administra-
" tion of the Lord's Supper he remained on his

F

" knees in the sacristy in front of the sanctissimum,
" which he had removed thither."

In another place the dean positively refused the
use of his church, on account of the impending conclusion of peace, when the mayor came forward and
met the chaplain in the market-place, and stated that
the dean had no right to refuse him, as the churches
were the property of the city. He sent to the
clergyman for the keys, had the church doors set
open, and he and the town council took part in the
service. They even asked the chaplain to lunch
with them after the service, in order to show their
desire to make amends for the dean's refusal.

Another priest granted the use of his church, with
the simple reservation that the entrance to the high
altar should be closed. Next morning, however, he
repented of his promise, and sent his assistant to
the commander, earnestly begging him not to profane
his church, for the bishop would have to be sent
for if a Lutheran service were conducted within its
walls. The officer, however, insisted, and a large
congregation assembled. Fortunately the Protestant

chaplain turned to the east on ascending the pulpit, and thus avoided giving a direct insult. In order to get there, however, he had to pass through two dull rooms, and up a dark staircase, and arriving at the top he found the pulpit door bolted, and in the darkness he could not find the bolt. The old sacristan would not assist him until he received a summary command to do so, as he evidently regarded the heretical preacher as an instrument of darkness, and remained behind in the sacristy, crossing himself and kneeling before a picture of St. Joseph.

CHAPTER V.

MORE FAVOURABLE OPPORTUNITIES OF PREACHING.

WE have spoken in a former chapter of the curious ℞and at the same time gratifying scenes which took place in many of the Roman Catholic churches of Austria. Our survey will, however, be incomplete were we to lose sight of those very interesting frontier lands which in past centuries bore such noble testimony to the truth. Notwithstanding the kind-nesses which the Protestant chaplains often received from the priests, and the many happy hours which they spent in their churches, it was always a source of great comfort when they came across any Protestant community. In the interior of Bohemia and Moravia such occasions were very rare, and it was only by some lucky chance that they ever discovered the little companies which remain as representatives of the reformed faith.   In the mountainous districts upon the frontiers these scattered communities are more numerous, and here the military chaplains had the further gratification of meeting with friends who though unknown were yet well known.   These little churches were generally known to the agents of the Gustavus Adolphus Society, and they used to convey the information to the army chaplains, and invite them to join their services.

Divisional Chaplain Rogge writes as follows respecting some of these small congregations in Bohemia, the only memorials still existing in his own land of the ever-blessed and memorable John Huss:—" While we were quartered for a week in " Raudnitz, in the splendid castle of Prince Lobko- " witz, I heard of the existence of two Protestant " communities at Krabschitz and Lipkowitz, which " are villages lying in the immediate neighbourhood. " Accompanied by my colleague, I employed the " first free day after our arrival in seeking them out.

" The pastors of these little communities received us
" with heart-stirring and overwhelming joy. Some
" of the troops of our division were quartered in both
" places, so we soon made arrangements for holding
" public worship. I appointed next Sunday for that
" purpose, including the celebration of the Lord's
" Supper, at the village of Lipkowitz. Bennesch,
" the worthy old pastor, was delighted at having the
" opportunity of joining in it. It was the first time
" for three months that I had preached in a Pro-
" testant place of worship, and it so happened that
" this one was built almost exclusively by charitable
" contributions received from Prussia. Protestant
" friends at Elberfeld had raised a considerable sum
" for building the neat little church, and several
" branches of the Gustavus Adolphus Society had
" also assisted in it. The chalice which I used on
" this occasion, instead of my field cup, was a present
" from the pupils of the Pforte School, sent by their
" late inspector, Niese. There I learnt the meaning
" of the words of our articles of belief as to the com-
" munion of saints, and experienced how far they

" override all the barriers of politics and nationali-
" ties, and unite in one household of faith those who
" have been brought together as enemies. Both I
" and my hussars, to whom I preached, felt quite at
" home in this church; and such was equally the
" case in the neat little town of Aussig, where I
" received a hearty welcome and enjoyed friendly
" intercourse in the house of Mr. A——, a manufac-
" turer, and one of the most respected members of
" this Protestant community. He had expressly
" offered to give lodging to the field chaplains of
" our faith, and next morning, when I was about to
" start at the appointed hour to walk to the church,
" which was at some distance, I found my host's
" handsome carriage at the door, ready to convey me
" thither. I should gladly have responded to his wish
" to have the communion celebrated at the church,
" had that been possible, as it was at that time
" without a stated minister, and could only be sup-
" plied occasionally by one from Teplitz; but I was
" obliged to hasten away in order to meet the bat-
" talions of the 1st regiment of Guards, which I had

" to visit on circuit prior to their approaching march
" back into their cantonments."

Another chaplain of division tells of a public
service and celebration of the Lord's Supper which
was held in the town hall of Pilsen, occupied by the
Protestants of the place whilst their own church, then
in course of construction, was being built. It was
being erected partly at the expense of the Gustavus
Adolphus Society of Saxony.   He writes in his
report : " Never has the Psalm of Luther, ' Ein feste
" ' Burg,' sounded so stirring to me, as in this
" armoury, converted into a house of God, whose
" walls were hung with rusty insignia of the Hussite
" and Thirty Years' wars, so much so that the band
" had to put their music-books on a cannon which
" had been captured by Wallenstein.   I have never
" preached with such an inward feeling of the power
" of the Gospel faith as here, where painful reminis-
" cences of the bloody religious wars surrounded me ;
" and I felt deeply moved when I realized the fact
" that these beautiful German and Slavic lands
" had been brought back again by force to the

" Roman Catholic church, and that down to the
" present day they can neither soar to spiritual
" nor material prosperity under the dominion of
" Austria."

The happiness which was experienced in their
communion with these interesting churches was
often much marred, however, by witnessing not only
the temporal, but also the spiritual necessities which
existed amongst them. In consequence of the
isolated position in which each community finds itself,
and its separation from the main streams of Protestant life, it is always in danger of pining away. The
incidental mention of a baptism, which a field chaplain had to undertake, indicates the rareness of such
an opportunity. In a report upon this matter, he
states : " In one of my circuits a Protestant inhabitant
" of a mountain village in Moravia asked me to
" baptise his child, as the nearest clergyman of his
" own faith was forty-seven (English) miles distant.
" Unfortunately the entire Protestant population of
" this village, which lay quite forgotten amongst the
" mountains, did not understand German; and in

" consequence of this, both at the baptism and the
" subsequent celebration of the Lord's Supper
" (which I held by special desire), I was obliged to
" avail myself of the services of a Jew, who acted as
" my interpreter, and who translated with great
" earnestness the confession of faith, the questions to
" the sponsors, the confession of sins," &c., &c.

Something more must, however, be said about the
internal arrangements of these services for the
troops, as we have hitherto rather dwelt upon the
externals.

The model generally followed during the campaign
was that prescribed officially for the military chaplains in time of peace, and which as a whole cannot
well be improved upon. The agenda prescribe a
short hymn at the beginning, then the liturgy, with
the reading of the Scriptures, on Sundays the Gospel
and Epistle of the day, and on the week days any
suitable Psalm, then a short sermon, followed by a
hymn, and concluding with the general church
prayers, or in their stead an extempore prayer, the
Lord's Supper and benediction. Under special cir-

cumstances, however, these had necessarily to be abbreviated.

The singing of the hymns was a matter of some difficulty, as the bandmasters were usually very badly supplied with sacred music, and it was therefore necessary to chose those hymns only which were adapted to the best-known tunes. More attention indeed should be directed to this matter, so that they might be supplied with at least six or eight suitable tunes; and it would be even still better if they were taught to play such tunes without notes. Many of the bands had no sacred music supplied to them, except such as was to be used at funerals. When the services were held in the Roman Catholic churches, they of course had the advantage of an organ; but unfortunately there was generally a difficulty in getting the organist, and even if he were willing to preside, the probability was that he was unacquainted with the proper chorales. A small tune-book will always be found a useful addition to the chaplain's library, but what is of greater importance, is that better regulations be made as to the supply of hymn-books to the soldiers. The want of these was one of the principal obstacles in the way of good vigorous singing on their part. As a rule, only those men who had served on the peace footing were supplied with such books, the rest of the several corps, together with the reserves and the Landwehr, being marched into the field without them. So small and useful an addition to their equipment should not be overlooked when making preparations for mobilisation. The leading of the responses in the liturgy was also a matter of some difficulty. In one regiment of the Guards they had a standing order to use the hautboys for their liturgical music, but this could not always be carried out. It has been suggested that the music for the responses should be bound up with the hymn-book, as there will always be found a sufficient number of soldiers to keep up the responses effectually, provided they were furnished with the notes. When occupying a Roman Catholic country it was all the more important that these matters should be well attended to ; and some chaplains varied the order of their services to some extent, with a special view to the population by which they were surrounded. The repetition of the general confession and of the creed always told upon them; and one of the chaplains remarks: "The summons, 'Let us profess " 'with the whole of Christendom our most holy " ' apostles' creed,' never failed to produce an evident " impresssion upon the inhabitants who came to hear. " I often observed how their dull-looking counten- " ances brightened up, and their attention became " doubly fixed."

Many too who have heretofore listened to the reading of the Gospel and Epistle of the day with in-difference, learnt during the war how precious those inspired words were, reminding them of their families at home, who would be hearing the same words at their respective churches. The clergy themselves also felt them more impressive than the sermons which they had to prepare very hurriedly, and under very unfavourable circumstances; and it was often remarked how frequently the lessons of the day, and especially the Psalms, were so suited to the situation of the moment that they needed no explanation or

application, but, on the contrary, appealed directly to
the consciousness of the hearers, or revealed the deeper
meaning of the most familiar passages.   God only
knows to how many the Book of Psalms has proved a
rich treasure.   How often the third Psalm has been
the most appropriate expression of the feeling which
filled the soldiers' hearts during the public services
held before the commencement of the campaign
when they were upon the march to the frontiers, who,
in reply to the opening complaint: "Lord, how are
" they increased that trouble me; many are they
" that rise up against me," could adopt the words of
the Psalmist: "I will not be afraid of ten thousands
" of people, that have set themselves against me
" round about."   At another time the fifth Psalm,
with its complaint against the vainglorious, was the
best answer they could give to their opponents.   How
fitting too the petitions in the seventh Psalm: "O
" Lord my God, in Thee do I put my trust; save me
" from all them that persecute me, and deliver me."
After the noble victories achieved by the Prussian
arms, the familiar Psalms of praise stirred up humble

and joyful thanks, and were the best antidotes to the pride which is so apt to spring up in the hearts of a victorious soldiery.

One of the chaplains reports that: "As we lay in "Swestar on the morning after the battle of König- "grätz, a captain summoned me to hold early prayers "with his company, which was bivouacked right in "front of the village church door. I was requested to "begin at once, for there was no time to be lost. The "sixty-sixth Psalm, selected as a Scripture reading, "furnished all that needed to be said on this morning "to those who had remained unhurt in the dangers of "the battle; and at the words: 'O, bless our God, ye "'people, and make the voice of His praise to be "'heard; which holdeth our soul in life, and suffereth "'not our feet to be moved; for Thou, O God, hast "'proved us; Thou hast tried us as silver is tried; "'Thou hast caused men to ride over our heads; we "'went through fire and through water, but Thou "'broughtest us out safe into a wealthy place,' I "saw tears of gratitude run down many cheeks." In such seasons as these God's word goes directly to the heart, and it needs but little addition on the part of man. It is a happy thing that it should be so, or the soldiers would have been badly off indeed. It was only towards the close of the war, when the army was scattered over a wide extent of country, that the field preacher had the chance of securing for his sole and separate use even the smallest quarters; and what are the opportunities for study at other times is well described by one of the chaplains who served in the Schleswig war: "If a chaplain has to dwell in a " farm-house with twenty or thirty soldiers, and share " a very small room with three or four of them, " the poor furniture of which must be turned out in " the evening in order to arrange beds for the night, " hours of quiet are looked upon as very rare and " valuable, and each moment of solitude as an inesti- " mable prize, in the midst of incessant urgings and " drivings, goings out and comings in." The carriages provided for them were at these times the best refuges for quiet meditation, and were so much used for the purpose that the officers frequently called them the "study." So long as the army was on the advance, the daily change of situation, the ignorance as to what the morrow might bring forth, and the short notices at which public services had generally to be held, compelled the chaplains usually to rest in faith upon the promise: "Take no thought how or " what ye shall speak, for it shall be given you in " that same hour what ye shall speak; for it is not " ye that speak, but the Spirit of your Father which " speaketh in you;" and under the special circumstances by which they were surrounded, they were certainly justified in doing so, while there is abundant evidence that they did not rest thereon in vain.

It is curious to observe how singularly appropriate to the occasion were many of the texts which were selected from the Gospel or Epistle of the day, in accordance with the usual custom in German churches. Thus, at Whitsuntide, when the whole Fatherland was stirred with the turmoil of the approaching war, there was the comforting promise: " Peace I leave with you; My peace I give unto " you." On the Second Sunday after Trinity, when the preparations for the war were all completed,

G

occurred the call, "Come, for all things are now ready."
Again, on the Third Sunday after Trinity, the apostolic warning: " Humble yourselves, therefore, under
" the mighty hand of God, that He may exalt you in
" due time; casting all your care upon Him, because
" He careth for you. Be sober, be vigilant," so
suited the circumstances in which the troops were
then placed, who were just about to cross the enemy's
frontiers, that it would have been difficult to have
selected anywhere a more appropriate passage of
Scripture: it served to encourage those who had
brought away with them so many cares about wife
and children, and whose hearts needed to be cheered
and lightened of their many burthens in order to
meet the approaching days with cheerfulness and
confidence. On the Fifth Sunday after Trinity, the
words " Launch out into the deep " sounded to them
as an inspiriting call, immediately preceding as it
did the great and decisive battle.

During the rapid advance through Moravia the
commissariat experienced great difficulty in procuring sufficient supplies for the bodily wants of the

army, as it traversed districts which had been already exhausted, and were in many places reduced to a wilderness; the Gospel for the Seventh Sunday after Trinity, with the account of the miraculous feeding of the four thousand, will not be readily forgotten by those who personally felt the force of the question: "Whence should we have so much bread " in the wilderness, as to fill so great a multitude?" Again, on the Tenth Sunday after Trinity, there occurred this passage: "If thou hadst known, even " thou, at least in this thy day, the things which " belong to thy peace—and the time of thy visita- " tion;" just at the time when the treaty of peace was being concluded, while on the other hand, the army was visited with the cholera, which told upon their ranks even far more than war. On the Fourteenth Sunday after Trinity, too, when the army was on the return march, the words: "Were there not " ten cleansed, but where are the nine? There are "not found that returned to give glory to God " save this stranger," must have suggested to the soldiers the true spirit which should animate them on their return home after being spared so many dangers.

It so frequently happened, however, that the public services were held on the week days besides or instead of the Sundays—for which there are no proper lessons appointed—that the chaplains had plenty of opportunity of selecting whatever texts seemed to them most appropriate for the time and circumstances. The military life and words of David readily supplied a large store of suitable passages, as well as such exhortations as, " Be thou faithful " unto death, and I will give thee a crown of life." On one occasion, when the army was pushing forward in hot haste, after the great battle of the 7th of July, the word of the Lord to Joshua, " There remaineth " yet very much land to be possessed," naturally suggested itself, and proved a source of encouragement to the soldiery. At another time, when on the march, " the pillar of cloud and the pillar of fire," which went before the hosts of Israel, reminded them of their dependence on the guidance of the Lord of Hosts. Sometimes, also, purely accidental circum-

stances determined the course of the preacher's
remarks. Those who have visited the more out-of-
the-way parts of Germany will have noticed that the
old wooden houses frequently have a verse of a Psalm
carved in the great beam which runs along the level
of the first floor; sometimes, too, these passages of
Scripture are highly decorated, so that the most
unobservant can scarcely fail to notice them. One of
the services was held in such a house, which had
been kindly placed by its proprietor at the disposal
of the chaplain; and over the door were the words,
in letters of gold, "The Lord God is a sun and
" shield, the Lord will give grace and glory." We
must also mention one other circumstance in connection with the selection of subjects for reflection, as it
was found, on comparing notes afterwards, that the
chaplains scattered about in the different quarters
had, as if by mutual consent, chosen the same text.
The army at that time was encamped on the Marchfeld, the most southern point of their expedition,
almost within sight of Presburg and Vienna, where
they were stopped in their progress by the interven-

tion of the armistice, which resulted in the conclusion of peace. "Ebenezer" was their watchword: and they simultaneously adopted the words of Samuel: "Hitherto hath the Lord helped us."

The military chaplains could not refrain, at times, from stirring up the patriotism of the soldiers under their charge, by a pointed reference to the historic associations of the places where they happened to be encamped. Central Germany has so often been turned into one vast battle-field, that it was quite a common occurrence for some portion of the army to be quartered on ground already consecrated with the blood of their ancestors. Almost every one of the battle-fields of Frederick the Great, in his three Silesian campaigns, were again trodden by the Prussian army, and the same villages furnished quarters to the troops. The names of Rossbach, Leuthen, and Torgau had naturally a special charm for them. At Hohenfriedberg they celebrated the anniversary of the battle on the very ground. At Brieg, adjoining the field of Mollwitz, the troops assembled for Divine worship and thanksgiving in the

Church of St. Nicholas, on the occasion of their first victory over the Austrians, where stands the tablet to the memory of Field-Marshal Von Geszler, the victor of Hohenfriedberg, who was buried there. In Bohemia, places were not lacking, such as Czaslau, Chotusitz, Prague, Collin, Lowositz, and Soor, which reminded them of former honours or reverses.

There were other circumstances of a special nature which demanded the consideration of the chaplains. At the outset they felt it their duty not only to teach the vital truths of Christianity, but also to strengthen the hearts of the men, and to infuse into them courage and enthusiasm.   They found this the more necessary, because immediately before the commencement of the campaign, doubts were very generally entertained as to whether there would be any actual warfare.   Many believed that there would be a peaceable settlement of all differences.   As an instance, a general of high rank, and one much esteemed, wrote his name in an album belonging to his hospitable host, adding to it this remark :

" Have been here during fourteen days of this
" imaginary war." In consequence of these delays
there was very little actual military enthusiasm pervading the army at the beginning of the campaign,
as compared with what was subsequently manifested,
and which increased daily after the beginning of
actual hostilities. Many during the earlier period
hoped to return home without fighting, and the
clergy, therefore, had to direct their preaching all
.the more to the great seriousness of the situation,
and to the struggle towards which they were then,
perhaps, drawing very near.

Even after the commencement of active operations, there was a calmness pervading the Prussian
soldiery which could not fail to be observed by those
who came into contact with them. A Saxon clergyman remarked to one of the army chaplains, as a
Pomeranian regiment was marching past his front
garden : " How quiet your people are ! they show no
" national enthusiasm; we should rather have sup-
" posed that they were under depressing circum-
. " stances." And this was by no means an uncommon

inference. The Saxons, in the simplicity of their nature, often sought to comfort them by promising to show kindness to them on their return; and there is no doubt about the fact that their enemies regarded it as an evidence of downheartedness. During this period the Austrian army distinguished itself by its boastful announcements, which found their way to the Prussians through the medium of the press.

At the close of the war the King acknowledged the services of the chaplains in the following terms: " My. clergymen, you have discharged an important " and difficult duty; I thank you for it. The cam- " paign has been short and glorious, and we partly " owe our victories to you, for the many prayers " offered to ¸God on our behalf. I know that at " home much prayer has been made for the success " of our arms. We must thank God upon our knees " that He has so speedily granted us such a result. " Preach to the people true humility, and no pride." These words, uttered in the presence of the army when encamped on the Marchfeld, and not without evident emotion on the part of the royal victor, were a sufficient refutation of the charge of pride, which was preferred against him by the Protestant clergyman at the Sebaldus Church at Nuremberg, in the presence of one of the Prussian chaplains ; which the latter quickly resented, saying that " high-" minded " would have been a more appropriate expression than " proud." They expressed, also, the general feeling which prevailed throughout the army, from the highest officer down to the meanest soldier. When the chaplain reminded some of the soldiers of the " King's Regiment " that they were much prayed for at home, they replied : " Yes, pastor, we tho-" roughly felt that such was the case in the hot days " of Nachod and Skalitz. The Austrians attributed " our success to our arms, but we know better ; it " was not our guns, but our Lord God who helped " us." A similar sentiment fell from the lips of an artilleryman, when the war was over, and the cap-tured guns were being ranged along the " Unter den " Linden " in Berlin, preparatory to the triumphal entry of the troops into the city. One of the chaplains, looking at the long row of cannon, asked him : " What do you say to all this ?" and his simple reply was : " Ah ! God was with us."

It must not, however, be inferred from these interesting details that such was the character of the whole army, and at all times. There is another side to the picture, and honesty requires that it shall not be passed unnoticed. The time of rest is always more fraught with danger to the soldier than the time of warfare. The Prussians, no less than others, were not proof against the allurements which appeared all the more enticing in comparison with the privations and fatigues which they had just experienced. Those portions of the army which remained for longer or shorter periods in Brünn and Prague were overtaken by sins of impurity to a grievous extent. The shamelessness with which prostitution spread itself in these cities was really shocking; and several of the chaplains were obliged to bear strong testimony against the moral dangers which threatened to overtake the troops.

Another danger is thus described by one of the

ministers: " The keeping of the seventh command-
" ment was fearfully neglected in consequence of
" forced levies being indispensable. In many of our
" soldiers the discipline into which they had been
" brought in time of peace, by the municipal and
" military regulations, was entirely lost. They took
" provisions wherever they found them, even when
" they were not pressed by hunger; and I must
" acknowledge that if the compulsory requisitions
" had lasted long the honour of the Prussian name
" would have been greatly tarnished. I sought to
" check this disorder both by censure and persuasion
" as far as my weak powers enabled me, and must
" own, with thankfulness to God, that I found many
" willing ears, and frequently heard strong ex-
" pressions of disapprobation on the part of the
" better intentioned, as to the shameless desires of
" their less scrupulous comrades. It was easy enough
" to observe how the natural heart of man is con-
" stituted, and how necessity quickly strips off all
" outward polish and culture. It is true that the
" wrongs which our troops here and there committed

" sink into insignificance in comparison with those
" which the Austrians, I say not, would have com-
" mitted in our land had they forced their way into
" it, but which they actually did commit amongst
" their own people. It frequently happened that
" we met with farm premises which were stripped
" by the enemy, who had fled from them, not only
" of food, but of all other valuable articles : an act
" but rarely perpetrated by our soldiers, and one
" which always entailed severe punishment. On
" the battle-field of Jicin I found a dead Austrian
" who had in his hand a woman's head-dress set
" with beautiful Bohemian stones, which had pro-
" bably been stolen from the neighbouring village
" of Unter-Lochow. It seemed to me to present
" a picture of fearful retribution." This state of
things is corroborated by one of the other chaplains, who says : " In consequence of the extraordi-
" nary forced marches, and the impossibility of fol-
" lowing with the stores as quickly as the troops
" advanced, the army was compelled to adopt forced
" levies for their provisioning, and this wrought so

" much evil that order and discipline were greatly
" endangered. The soldiers, finding their needs
" increasing, not only began to make demands upon
" their own authority, but the subalterns and
" gens-d'armes who were interposed against it re-
" fused obedience. Many grievous excesses resulted,
" and we were ordered to take notice of them in
" the sermons at the next public worship."

So long as the troops were upon the advance, and
were engaged in actual warfare, there was little drunk-
enness amongst them; but when the armistice took
place this vice made its appearance here and there;
and it was necessary to direct some words to the
consciences of the soldiers upon the subject, and
to warn them against lurking temptation in this
quarter.

It was also useful during the last few weeks to
review petty jealousies by the light of God's word,
for certain portions of the troops boasted of special
honour and deeds of heroism, and quarrelled openly
with others over this or that point, when either
portion of the army would have brought about the

same result. The reports in the newspapers—evidently written frequently by unauthorized and ignorant correspondents, whose information was very partial—often produced disputes, and never served to promote a spirit of good-fellowship in the army.

To counteract these various evils, a few words in the sermon were sometimes appropriate, though such subjects were not always agreeable to handle. Some of the officers desired the ministers to regard them as "Noli me tangere." For instance, it is stated in one of the reports: "In the neighbour- " hood of F—— a wine-cellar was broken into by " night. I considered it my duty to speak against " such an act in my sermon, and to awaken moral " disgust at it. As I had heard from certain por- " tions of the troops that sundry soldiers belonging " to their regiment had been guilty of the said bur- " glary, I mentioned the circumstance in a public " service, which excited bitter remarks from the " colonel of the regiment. He said, 'If my men do " 'not profit by being punished for the offence, " 'nothing will be attained by your preaching.' A

" correspondence arose, but ultimately peace was
" restored between us." In such cases as these the
position of a conscientious chaplain was one of great
delicacy, and it required good tact and wise fore-
sight in administering such occasional censures.

Notwithstanding such instances as these, the
field preachers generally bear most favourable testimony as to the ready reception of the truth. There
was a joyful participation in public worship, and
the troops usually paid marked attention to the
sermons. In this respect, however, a great difference
was naturally to be met with between the various
regiments and divisions. Some showed much more
interest in and inward perception of the truth than
others, and in this respect the influence of the
officers, and especially the superior ones, was
quite unmistakable. Regiments might be named
where God-fearing principles could be recognized
at a glance, and where Christian discipline was
readily discernible. In such, not only did a larger
number out of their ranks take part in Divine service
of their own free will, but a greater earnestness

could also be traced in all their countenances. It was easier, too, to arrange for public worship with some portions of the troops than with others. Difficulties which in one case often frustrated the holding of the service were in another case not experienced, or readily set aside. In one regiment or battalion the somewhat late announcement of the public service was always circulated in time, whereas in another whole companies were often ignorant of such being held. Whilst in one the officers were always present in full numbers, in another only those who were ordered to attend in their official capacity made their appearance; and that such should have been the case in any regiment is the more to be regretted, as it was observed that the greater or less interest of the troops was always in proportion as their spiritual welfare was respected on the part of the officers.

Many of the chaplains received the thanks of the commanders, and sometimes of the whole regiment, for the manner in which they had discharged their responsible duties; and while acknowledging

H

that much of the feeling and susceptibility of the troops would be evanescent, and due to the special circumstances, privations, and dangers to which at the moment they might be subject, it was generally felt by them that no minister can find a more favourable sphere of labour than a military congregation in the field.

CHAPTER VI.

THE LORD'S SUPPER.

HAVING entered at some length into the varied incidents of preaching to the army when occupying
the enemy's country, we must devote a short space
to those which specially affected the celebrations of
the Lord's Supper during the same period. These
occasions were not without their special interest. It
was generally felt desirable to supplement the ordinary public worship with the communion service,
and at the commencement of the campaign it was
often held instead of simple prayer-meetings, at the
special repuest of the soldiers themselves. Previously
to the march into the enemy's country, and during
the days of active warfare, the soldiers of a whole

regiment or battalion, together with their officers, often joined in the Lord's Supper, and such were always very elevating services. Often even the Roman Catholic soldiers would not allow themselves to be excluded, and presented themselves to take part in the Protestant sacrament, when there may have been no priest of their own persuasion at hand. On this matter one of the chaplains says: " Before I went into the church, a junior officer " asked me, in the name of some Roman Catholics, " whether they might be allowed to join in our " service, for we were then about to celebrate the " Lord's Supper. I replied, 'I had no objection, " ' because our Saviour said, " Drink ye all of it." " ' The use of the cup was therefore not only not " ' wrong, but was a command of Christ, and all must " ' act according to their consciences.' They accord- " ingly came."

It was necessary, however, even with the Protestants, to warn them against any superstitious use of this ordinance, for amongst them such ideas were found to be much more prevalent than would generally be supposed. There were many of the so-called "patents" sold in Silesia, which, when worn on the breast, are believed to render the wearers cut, thrust, and ball proof. Some of the officers even rather encouraged such superstitious practices, saying: "Such an amulet is a very practical thing: " if a man believes in it, he goes much more " readily into the fire, and that is the principal " matter. Whether it results from faith or super-" stition is all the same: the belief makes him " happy." Amongst the Pomeranian soldiers all sorts of recommendations were given as to how to ward off the bullets of the enemy when in battle. An old Jew, out of thankfulness and attachment to his former countryman, brought a snake's head to a Prussian colonel as an amulet. In Bohemia many charms came into the possession of the soldiers, which were carried in little oblong boxes suspended round the neck by a string, or on the inner portion of the flap of the knapsack. Upon them were written: "In the name of the Holy "Trinity † † †, of the Blessed Virgin †, thou shalt

" go without injury and danger.   Jesus help †,
" St. Florian help †, St. Peter help †, so that no
" bullet shall be able to hurt me."

The celebration of the Lord's Supper was often
beset with practical difficulties. After crossing the
enemy's frontiers, the providing of sufficient bread
and wine for the larger communion services was no
easy matter. For the former it was found highly ad-
vantageous to be plentifully supplied with wafers,
which were much more convenient in the field than
the bread generally used at other times, being so
portable that no one need incur the risk of running
short. Wine was often not to be had either for
love or money. In Pardubitz, some days after the
battle of Königgrätz, Chaplain Rogge had to go into
all the wine-stores and public-houses for some bottles
of wine; and it needed great management to get
hold of any, as they were carefully concealed, and
none would own to having any supply to sell, because
they suspected that it would be taken away by
order, and that the promise of payment was only a
pretence; there was accordingly nothing else to be

done but to use some of the forced contributions of
wine for this as well as ordinary purposes. A chaplain could always carry wine enough in his carriage
for a limited number of communicants; but when
they assembled in hundreds, and even in thousands,
it would have needed a special waggon to carry it.
At one celebration of the Lord's Supper, which was
held in front of Königinhof, two days before the
battle of Königgrätz, nearly eighty bottles of wine
were used. For these large gatherings it was not
always easy to be sure of having a sufficiency, as
there was no list given in of intending communicants, which, under such circumstances, would have
unnecessarily increased the already onerous duties of
the regimental secretaries; and the best criterion
the chaplain could go by was to watch the consump-
tion of wafers. It was very rarely they were em-
barrassed by the supply of wine failing, and at a
service in the field it did not occasion the annoyance
which it would have done under other circumstances.
It appears from the complaints of the chaplains that
they are not free from red-tapeism in the Prussian

service, even in the matter of sacramental wine. The clergy are required to furnish the commissariat with vouchers for all moneys they have disbursed in payment for bread and wine; and considering the difficulties above described of procuring wine at all, it is not to be wondered at that this was simply impossible; moreover, in Bohemia, the poor people scarcely understand German, and, even if they know the language, it is difficult to teach them how to prepare a proper voucher.

In the large services spoken of above, it was absolutely necessary to depart from the routine usual in German churches; the plan of repeating the formulary to each company of six or eight as they consecutively advance to the altar had to be abolished, which would have occupied far too much time, and would have been wearisome both to the minister and the communicants. Some discussion has arisen as to the propriety of holding such open-air services for this purpose, it being argued that religious feeling is violated, and that the decorum, which should be strictly regarded in such a festival, cannot be preserved. But it must not be forgotten that, what would be very improper under other circumstances, may be the decorum of war. It would pain any one to see in a churchyard at home the body of the poorest man lowered into a speedily-dug hole, which scarcely deserves the name of a grave, without any coffin, and barely clad; but in war such is thought natural enough. In like manner, also, if the Lord's Supper be celebrated in the field in a different style from what it is at home, it will, and should, not violate any religious feeling; everything that is by rule, and even all the customs of Christendom, have an end at such times. If the Christians of the first centuries were able to celebrate the Lord's Supper to edification in the catacombs, and the Waldenses and Huguenots of later times in forests and defiles, the soldier who from his heart wishes for the heavenly food, perhaps just before his last battle, will find a departure from the rule adopted at home quite natural and even welcome; and the service will perhaps rather assist in promoting his edification than take away from it, just because it forcibly reminds him of the extraordinary nature of his situation. It is satisfactory to know that there is abundant evidence that these services were especially quickening. A few extracts from the chaplains' reports will sufficiently establish this. The first is written by a minister attached to the Army of the Maine, and the scene is the battle-field of Helmstadt. " The drum-altar was erected under a large " tree on the border of the forest; the regiment " stood in the form of a horseshoe on the mountain " slope, the band at my side. The echo of our " singing and the chorale sounded remarkably sweet, " especially whilst the band played ' Jesus, my trust,' " during the celebration of the Lord's Supper. There " were nearly six hundred who took part in the com- " munion. Two hundred men, in double file, stepped " forwards simultaneously, forming themselves into a " half-circle ; a soldier accompanied me, carrying a " jug of wine, as I passed up and down the ranks, and " in this way the service proceeded rapidly. Those " who had partaken of the supper sat quietly in the " shade at the border of the forest, and at the con-

" cluding prayer closed in again in a large circle
" round the altar. It was the most impressive
" celebration of the Lord's Supper that I have ever
" witnessed. Some of the officers stepped up to me
" with tears in their eyes, and acknowledged that,
" since their confirmation, they had never been so
" moved by any communion service as by this
" one on the field of battle." The great gathering in the forest of Königinhof, which has already
been referred to, is thus described by the celebrant:
" Nearly two thousand men took part in this service,
" and the dispensing of it occupied more than three
" hours. In order not to weary the communicants
" too much, nor to weaken the impression of the
" service by making it too long, I requested the
" commanders to let the men lie upon the grass
" after the close of the Confession and the Liturgy
" preceding the communion. Then each one hun-
" dred men stepped forward in two ranks in a half-
" circle, and the dispensing of the elements went
" forward quietly and without any undue haste.
" As soon as the communicants of one battalion had

" received the bread and wine I dismissed them with
" a benediction.   Under the circumstances in which
" we found ourselves in those days, such a celebra-
" tion of the communion in large numbers had its
" special signification." The evidence of the soldiers
themselves is also to the same effect. A grenadier,
who subsequently died of his wounds, wrote home to
his relatives after a communion service, saying :
" To-day, at the close of public worship, we partook
" of the Holy Sacrament, and I went back to my
" tent in order to offer up a short prayer to Heaven,
" in firm faith in our Almighty God, who doeth all
" things well."   Another wrote to his parents : " Yes-
" terday we had preaching in the field, and after-
" wards Chaplain R—— administered the Lord's
" Supper, in which I also took part. ˙Ah! would
" that I had been able to go at that moment into
" the heat of battle !   I felt myself so mightily
" inspirited, and the thought of dying for my father-
" land was so glorious to me, that my tears fell,
" and I vowed anew to fight like a good Christian
" and a brave soldier."

CHAPTER VII.

ON THE BATTLE-FIELD.

LET us now accompany the chaplains to the actual fields of battle, and see the nature of the duties which devolved upon them at such times. When a battle was imminent, the chaplains needed to leave their carriages behind in the column, and to join the staff of their respective divisions on horseback, so as to be at hand immediately their services were required. Any relaxation of this rule was apt to entail some loss of usefulness, and might even put the clergyman himself in some personal danger. One of those in the Army of the Maine got himself into a very awkward scrape by not strictly adhering to this regulation. Field Preacher Siebold, who was attached to the 13th division, felt himself con-

strained to remain for a while behind with the
wounded in Kissingen, whilst his division advanced
towards Würzburg and Aschaffenburg. As he
subsequently hastened on after the troops, with the
idea that the route from Kissingen to Aschaffenburg was open, he came unexpectedly upon a Bavarian regiment of light cavalry at Hammelburg,
with Prince Luitpold of Bavaria in command.
Siebold stopped for a few moments at the hospital
to see General Schachtmeier, who was wounded,
leaving his servant standing before the door with
his saddle horse: the man had the red cross on his
arm, while the chaplain wore the well-known blue
and white scarf. The prince asked to see his authority, which was most willingly produced for his
inspection. He found it satisfactory, and added,
" You may pass through." No sooner had the
prince said this, than he noticed the stately horse
that belonged to the field preacher, and had it taken
away. The minister calmly remonstrated against
this, appealing to the Geneva compact. But the
prince replied, abruptly, " The horse is branded, and

" not private property; it belongs to the King of
" Prussia, and is, therefore, a prize of war." All the
pleadings of the field preacher, and the reference he
made to the services which he had rendered to
the Protestant Bavarians in the hospitals were of
no avail. The prince answered, "You hold an
" office which is indeed honourable, and in which I
" wish you God's blessing, but—the horse belongs
" to me." He further added: "The Prussians have
" taken away the horse belonging to my adjutant,
" and, therefore, I must hold myself blameless as to
" this." Some of the officers also said, ironically,
" Parson, you will find walking more agreeable
to you than riding." There was nothing for him
but to yield, and go forward on foot, and pick
up such conveyance as he could find. Unfortunately, poor Siebold's troubles did not end here.
As he went on his way, he met a Bavarian company
bivouacked before Gemünden, the captain of which
once more stopped the field preacher. His papers,
which were found to be sufficient by Prince Luitpold,
did not satisfy the inferior officer, and he had

him conducted to the commander of the regiment, amidst the scornful laughter of the populace, who suspected him of being a spy. Here a thorough search of his coat-pockets took place; innocent letters, postage-stamps, &c., were detained, and the pretended spy was finally taken into custody under escort, and kept for two days and two nights under lock and key, whilst his servant had to live in jail on bread and water. During the night the troops removed their quarters; but a policeman was left to guard the door until the Prussians came; whereupon he disappeared suddenly, and the prisoners were released. Only one other instance occurred of a chaplain having the misfortune of being put in confinement for a short time, and that occurred during the armistice: the volunteer Field Preacher Sheffer was taken prisoner by the Austrian hussars as he was going from Iglau towards Znaim to visit the hospital; and, after three days' detention, he was sent to the latter place and dismissed, the Prussians being quartered in the immediate neighbourhood of that town.

Notwithstanding all their endeavours, the chaplains did sometimes miss opportunities of great usefulness. For instance, on the occasion of the battle of Gitschin, which took place sooner than he expected, Divisional Chaplain Brandt, of the 2nd corps d'armée, was, through a misunderstood order, kept in his carriage in the rear for some hours. After hurrying forward as rapidly as possible, he only reached the' scene of battle at midnight, when the engagement was over, having had the painful sensation of witnessing from a distance the smoke of the powder, which told him that his people were dying without his being able to get near them. He and other clergymen, who more or less felt this difficulty, recommend that their carriage should at such times immediately follow the light field hospital, which takes its place behind the vanguard, especially as it will then be at hand at the dressing places, and can carry some little supply of refreshment, which is so necessary for the wounded. This suggestion is not made for the sake of dispensing with the saddle horse, because it often happens that when a battle takes place the troops strike into the woods, where the hospital and carriage cannot follow.

Whenever possible, the chaplains rode forward with the officers to the front, as there was generally a brief interval before the commencement of the engagement, which they could profitably employ; and at these times the soldiers always heard them gladly. Short services were often held on such occasions. Thus, before the battle of Münchengrätz, as the 14th brigade, which had been appointed to storm the high Muskiberg, and so turn the extreme right wing of the enemy, was stationed in a corn-field before the town of Turnau, the commander gave a short and solemn exhortation, the troops sang the hymn, "Ach bleib mit deiner Gnade," and the chaplain said a few words on the text 1 John iii. 16, concluding with prayer and the benediction. Just as the last notes of the parting chorale were dying away, the hollow booming of cannon was heard in the distance, and the brigade advanced with quick step to the scene of struggle. Again, on the 28th

June, Divisional Chaplain Rogge availed himself of
the brief interval when the troops under his spiritual
care were being drawn up in array for the battles of
Burgersdorf and Soor. He thus describes the
scene: " The vanguard was marched out through
" the defile of Eipel, and the single battalions
" prepared themselves for the attack upon the
" enemy, who were still lying in bivouac at about an
" hour's walking distance. The arrival of the
" remaining troops had to be waited for ere the
" order to advance could be given. I made use
" of this interval of time to address a word of en-
" couragement to the troops who were appointed to
" take the front of the battle. I rode forward to
" the battalions, which were now formed in columns,
" and held a short service with each of them, com-
" mencing with a Psalm or other passage of Scrip-
" ture, and concluding with prayer. The texts
" selected were very appropriate to the situation,
" such as, ' I will look up to the hills, from whence
" ' cometh my help: my help cometh from the
" ' Lord, who made heaven and earth;' or the

" promise, ' They that wait upon the Lord shall
" ' renew their strength; they shall mount up with
" ' wings as eagles; they shall run and not be weary ;
" ' they shall walk, and not faint.' Words like
" these, uttered within sight of the banners already
" unfurled for the battle, could not fail to produce
" a deep impression. Tears glistened in many eyes,
" and some of the soldiers fell upon their knees in
" devout emotion. The firing of the first cannon
" coincided, as if by arrangement, with the Amen to
" the last prayer. Since the close of the war many
" have assured me that that morning service before the
" battle will remain indelibly fixed on their memory."

It was rarely that such a good opportunity as this
occurred; and frequently the assault followed so
quickly, that the batteries had scarcely opened fire,
or the battalions were deployed into fighting columns,
ere the murderous struggle began. The minister's
place was then no longer in front of the troops, but
at the dressing places of the wounded in the rear,
though the excitement of the moment did sometimes carry them away from their special duties.

One of the Roman Catholic chaplains was even to be seen in the field of Königgrätz, dressed in the green cap of a sharpshooter and high cavalry boots, at one moment taking an Austrian officer prisoner, and then directly after rushing from one wounded man to another to administer to him the extreme unction. Such, however, was not strictly their business—to be amongst the wounded and the dying, to spare no privations and no fatigue—to withdraw from no discouraging sights, to have an open ear for all complaints, and a ready hand to help, even if the work be distasteful and troublesome—to be a true friend to the unfortunate, and enter into their individual cases—to call the surgeon and the hospital assistants to a place where, perhaps, the wounded have remained lying overlooked, is the glorious duty of the chaplain on the field of battle. Not that these services even can be rendered without some display of personal valour. Many instances of immediate danger appear in their reports. The chaplains were not unfamiliar with the peculiar whirr of shells flying overhead, or with the sight of them falling

and bursting around them, or penetrating the houses
and farmsteads where they were staying with the
wounded. Moreover, it is well known that the white
flags with the red cross upon them were little respected by the Austrians, and, indeed, could not
always be distinguished on such wet days as the
morning of the 3rd of July.

The duties of the chaplains at the dressing places
of the wounded were rather temporal than spiritual.
Occasionally one meets with a dangerously-wounded
man, who feels the nearness of death, and asks for
the consolations of the Gospel, and the offering up of
a prayer on his behalf, or at all events accepts the
same with thankfulness; others may be found who
are desirous of the Lord's Supper. In administering
this the Protestant chaplains were more reserved
than their Roman Catholic brethren, who, unasked
and unbidden, hastened to ensure the safety of all
who were badly wounded by means of extreme
unction; but when the desire was expressed, this last
service of love often became one of the most delightful duties of their office. The worst cases naturally

fell to their lot, as the surgeons usually handed over
to their care those amongst the wounded whose end
was evidently at hand.

In general, the first hours after receiving wounds
are the least suited for the direct work of the chaplain. Most of the sufferers are at such a time too
much engaged with themselves and their bodily
condition. Moreover, they generally lie in such
close proximity that the surgeons and chaplains
could hardly avoid jostling each other, and the loud
cries and moans (which were particularly common
amongst the Austrians) rendered quiet intercourse
impossible. A few friendly words of sympathy and
encouragement, coupled with an inquiry as to the
nature of the injury received, was all that was possible; and even this was not without beneficial
effect. There are, however, many other ways in
which he can make himself useful, and at the same
time win his way to the hearts of the sick men.
Nothing is so acceptable to them as to receive refreshing drinks, and many have been the thanks,
both from friend and foe, for such a comfort. The

church of Chlum was filled with hundreds of men,
who were wounded at the great battle of Königgrätz,
and who were lying in the aisles and pews; and the
constant cry, from one end of the church to the
other, was for water. While refilling the glass one
was beset on all sides with, "Reverend sir, let me
"have some; pray give me some!" and the chaplains could not supply it fast enough, as they had to
fetch it themselves in bottles and pails from the
wells in the neighbourhood. The chaplains often
met with men who were lying uncomfortably upon
their temporary mattrasses, and who, without assistance, could not put themselves into a more convenient position. Another soldier might be met
with who was half-famished, and whose thankfulness
for even a small piece of bread would be testified
by a hearty "God bless you, sir!" Then those
whose hours were numbered had frequently some
message to send to the wife at home, or to the
parents or sisters—perhaps it was the last kiss of
love—and the writing materials had to be got as
quickly as possible, to take down their words, and to

write the address. One grenadier, who was severely wounded, sent the following simple message to his wife: " If I do not return, bring up the child in the " fear of God, and pray diligently with him." An Austrian family remains to this day without any tidings of one of its members, who was a captain in that army, except what was sent them by one of the Prussian chaplains. Many of the wounded deposited their last ready money in the hands of the ministers, to be forwarded to their dear ones at home in case of death. Others, who were only slightly wounded, but were nevertheless unable to write at first, have been greatly comforted when the chaplains have undertaken to write to their relatives, and thus anticipated all exaggerated reports.

While the clergy busied themselves in this manner, the army was still pushing forward, and the scene of actual fighting had, perhaps, considerably changed its ground, which compelled the chaplains to follow. The freshly wounded were continually being brought in from the field to the temporary hospitals; but it

was impossible they could attend to all; and some
poor fellows were not even discovered till the second
or third day. The ministers frequently came across
such, and all they could do was to wet their parched
lips and keep them from starvation while they went
to fetch ambulances for them. Doubtless, many
perished for want of any help, while many, alas!
were ill-treated and plundered by the wretches who
followed in the wake of the army for the sake of
booty. There were, however, some glorious exceptions to this rule, and we cannot help mentioning
one instance of heroic devotion on the part of a
Good Samaritan, who regarded not danger in an
errand of mercy. A soldier had been lying for
some hours in a state of unconsciousness on the
battle-field of Königgrätz, and when he came to himself again it was quite dark. He saw nothing but
bloody heaps of corpses, and, as far as his eye could
reach, there was not a living being to be seen. He
believed himself near to death, when suddenly a
young girl appeared with a large bottle of wine in
her hand; and as soon as she saw the sick man she

gave him some to drink, and washed and bound up
his wounds. In this manner she refreshed many of
the soldiers who were left lying where they fell;
and then she went onwards, promising to procure, if
possible, the necessary means for conveying them
away. Of her we may truly say, "Go, and do
"thou likewise."

In order, however, to give a more complete
picture of what were the labours of the chaplains at
the time of active engagements, let us take a few
extracts from their own reports. The first describes
the scene at the dressing places during the battle
of Nachod. "I found," he says, "two or three
"surgeons, who were much in request, as the
"wounded arrived in large numbers. I endeavoured
"to assist them. There was an officer of the 37th
"regiment, whose right hand was shattered, but
"who, nevertheless, taking the sword in his left,
"had persevered in his command. Then a fusileer
"of the same regiment looked at me with tearful
"eyes; he was shot through the neck. I blessed
"him: he then wrote some lines to his parents, full

" of pious resignation, which were intermixed with
" the Roman Catholic salutation, 'Praised be Jesus
" ' Christ.' A lieutenant of the 8th regiment of
" dragoons was shot through the foot: he dictated
" some words to me to be sent to his wife. Having
" left the house where he and several other wounded
" were lying, I was startled by the sudden appear-
" ance of four or five horses: they had no saddles
" on, and were immediately followed by a mêlée of
" dragoons and Uhlans, who had been repulsed.
" One Uhlan released himself from his horse with
" difficulty, and sank down, as I thought, in a dying
" state. The number of wounded now increased
" rapidly, Austrians and Prussians all mixed together.
" Spiritual consolation and brief converse was held
" out to the brethren ; but the true work to be
" done was that of the Good Samaritan. The heat
" was terrible. Supplicating cries for water were
" heard in every direction, and other restoratives
" were not at hand. I consequently turned water-
" carrier for some hours. As I went round the
" corner of a hill to fetch it, shells struck close by

" me three or four times. I spent a portion of the
" afternoon amongst the wounded in the hospitals
" of the town. There I met Count R——, and pre-
" pared him for death. Near him lay a young
" Austrian, of whose recovery the surgeon gave but
" little hope, and who met death with the joyful
" consciousness that he had maintained his sworn
" allegiance to the Emperor, even to the end. As
" evening approached, there were increasing calls for
" activity in imparting spiritual consolation and
" bodily assistance, both at the dressing place and at
" the hospital in the town. Very early next day I
" renewed my wanderings. I wrote several letters
" for General von O——, who was wounded : subse-
" quently I succeeded in buying some bottles of
" wine ; and with them I hastened to the field of
" battle of the preceding day, in order to revive a
" little the wounded men who were still lying about.
" Most of them were Austrians. In one part I found
" many dead and wounded of the regiment ' Deutsch-
" ' meister ;' their groans and cries were heart-
" rending. The poor men were most imperfectly

" sheltered from the sun's rays. One sufferer begged
" me to remove a dead body, which was lying by
" his side; another entreated me to see if he could
" be conveyed into the town. The few mouthsful
" of wine that I was able to offer to those unfor-
" tunates were accepted with heartfelt thankfulness."
Again, at the battle of Skalitz, the troops of the
same division were again under fire; and he says:
" Where the railway touches upon the road, I found
" a large number of wounded Austrians, who begged
" for water. Laden with their field-flasks and
" cooking utensils, I went to a house at about a
" quarter of an hour's distance, in hope of finding
" water. There I met with more wounded men,
" and amongst them an adjutant of the 58th regi-
" ment, and Colonel von W——, for whom I wrote
" to his wife. Though my help was still needed at
" this place, I was obliged to return to my languish-
" ing Austrians, to refresh them, and to cool their
" wounds."

The divisional chaplain of the 4th corps d'armée
thus describes the scene in the neighbourhood of

Czerekwice: " When the first of the wounded sol-
" diers were brought in, we accompanied them into
" the Schloss, which was at once converted into a
" hospital. As soon as the chief of the surgical staff
" saw us, he summoned us to help him to establish
" order. I had scarcely complied with this summons
" ere I discovered that bodily help was the first
" necessity here. I accordingly made up the beds
" for many hours together, put the wounded and the
" ambulances to rights, helped to bind up the
" broken limbs, &c., finding at the same time rare
" opportunities here and there of dropping a few
" words of spiritual comfort and exhortation. I re-
" member particularly a conversation that I had with
" a wounded officer, who has since gone to sleep in
" the Lord. He sent his servant to fetch me; and
" said, ' I feel I am mortally wounded. My sins,
" ' which are, and have been, many, grieve my heart';
" ' and I wish that I could begin a new life. Ah! I
" ' lived carelessly in my youth; but now I would
" ' that I had lived differently.' I pointed out to
" him the mercy of God, and the cross of Christ, and

" asked him whether he believed in the forgiveness
" of sins through the atoning blood of the Saviour.
" He said, ' Yes, I believe.' Thereupon I assured him
" with all the blessed consolations that the word of
" God extends to hearts that are truly penitent. He
" remained quite quiet for a time, and then termi-
" nated the conversation from sheer exhaustion,
" saying, ' I wish to die ; but even though I may still
" ' live, pray for me.' At four o'clock I went to the
" battle-field, after begging a morsel of bread in the
" village ; for I could not help feeling that the sol-
" diers still lying outside must remain there through-
" out the night, as the castle and all the houses in
" the village were already full. It was a fearful
" sight ; some hundreds of dead and wounded were
" lying in the forest and on the field of battle.
" Again we were obliged to combine spiritual
" teaching and bodily help. M—— and I seized all
" the Austrian camp-kettles, procured water, and
" held it to the burning lips of the poor men, who
" were clamouring to be taken to the hospital, or
" intreating Joseph and Mary to help them, while

" the country people paid no attention. I often had
" to take away the cloak from some dead body lying
" hard by, to cover up the wounded, who complained
" bitterly of the cold, for which I was often rewarded
" with a most impressive look of thankfulness."

Near to the same spot, in the direction towards
Dohalica, where the bold Pomeranians had determi-
nately withstood a hail of grenades for a whole hour
in the gardens of the village, two field preachers of
the 2nd corps d'armée met together, one of them
carrying bottles of wine, followed by a sexton with
drinking water. They joined company, and went to
a station where the most horrible misery reigned.
The church was full of prisoners, wounded and dead.
There were about one hundred wounded in the
school-house, and, practically, but one surgeon and
one assistant to attend to them. The ministers
hardly knew where to begin. Straw and water were
needed, but their supply of the latter was only like
a few drops of rain falling on the parched ground;
they were nevertheless thankful to be able to refresh
somé few thirsty ones; and amidst the cries and

K

bustle that prevailed everywhere they strove to
impart also a word from God. They were obliged,
however, to desist from sheer physical exhaustion
and heart-sickness at the terrible scenes before
them. The whole place was covered with human
blood, and the bodies of the dead, the dying, the
hideously mutilated, and the slightly wounded, all
lying indiscriminately together. These were hard
times, even for those who had the strongest nerves
and the strongest constitutions.

Another chaplain thus describes a halt upon the
battle-field of Königgrätz : " For four days I wan-
" dered from morning till evening amongst the
" invalids, knelt by the side of their straw, wiped
" the blood from the face of one, arranged a bed for
" another, asked sympathetically after their wounds,
" and attended to all kinds of wishes, prayed with
" many in a loud voice, so that those lying around
" might hear, and directed all to the only physician
" and helper, Jesus Christ, commending every heart
" that needed rest to find it alone in the living and
" life-giving word of God. This mode of rendering

" service was always welcome. Some of the soldiers
" thanked me by holding out their hands; and I
" could read in the eyes of others how suitably the
" words from God's own book applied to them. I
" asked a Saxon, Captain Von G——, if I could be
" of any service to him. He replied, 'Pray with
" ' me.' I did so, and made earnest supplication to
" God on his behalf. When I had ended, he drew
" a long breath, and said, 'That is refreshing: that
" ' brings peace.' I generally asked about those at
" home, and offered to put in writing any words that
" might be dictated to me. Water had to be brought
" from an hour's distance, and we prepared our
" coffee, which was all the refreshment we had that
" day, in the horse-trough. I had the satisfaction of
" giving away many small glasses of wine, the only
" stimulant we had on the spot. An Austrian cap-
" tain of a cavalry regiment appeared much ex-
" hausted, so I handed him a fragment of ship biscuit
" and a small glass of wine, at which he shed tears
" of thankfulness, and blessed me again and again,
" as if I had rendered him an unspeakable service.

" I found all the soldiers ready to accept my New
" Testaments, Psalms, Prayer-books, and tracts ; and
" very often I heard a voice calling to me for one
" from some remote corner of a barn.   When I
" handed to Lieutenant Von S——— a New Testament,
" he drew his own out of his litter, saying, ' My good
" ' mother gave me this.'   The constantly-repeated
" experiences of human suffering under amputation
" and in cries of pain, coupled with the incessant
" labour of teaching and imparting spiritual consola-
" tion, strained our courage and nerves in an extra-
" ordinary degree.   Nevertheless I cannot think of
" these days without thanking God for the wonderful
" strength with which I was able to accomplish my
" delightful work ; though I fully realized the utter
" inability of coping with such labours unaided from
" above."

These extracts will serve to afford some idea as to
the nature of the work which is before the military
chaplain in time of war.   The experiences are har-
rowing to the feelings ; but he always has the satisfaction of knowing that if he is not serving a higher

purpose, he is at all events welcome as the admi-
nistrator of bodily comfort. Curious cases even of
this occur in their reports. Once a minister went
into a barn filled with men who were badly wounded,
when he saw an Austrian just before him who was
shot through the breast, and who was trying in the
intervals between his painful spasmodical gaspings
to drag off his cloak, which was covered with blood.
No one could understand him, until at last his
object was discovered; the pocket of the cloak containing twenty cartridges, the weight of which
greatly aggravated the poor man's sufferings every
time he drew breath. Another was going over a
field of battle administering restoratives to the
wounded, when he came across a Prussian soldier
who was shot through the mouth, and was lying on
the ground quite exhausted from loss of blood.
Thick coagulum covered his lips, and when the
minister bade him take a drink of wine, he replied,
"Thank you very much, but I shall make your
" cup dirty;" an answer which almost moved
the chaplain to tears, while at the same time

such an instance of self-denial taught him a great
lesson.

In Western Germany, where the Army of the
Maine carried on their operations, the same experiences met the ministers attached to the troops.
One of them describes the great Kursaal of Kissingen, so well known to those who seek the benefit
of its waters, as having been crowded with the
wounded, even all along the corridors which stretch
right and left of the entrance; and while the Roman
Catholic priests were administering absolution and
the extreme unction, he was going from bed to bed
and declaring out of the Gospel the only way of
salvation through Christ. Amongst other cases of
interest, he mentions : " A young Protestant Christian
" called me to his side : God's Spirit had shown him
" the need of repentance, and he wept bitterly as he
" related how he, the son of a pious schoolmaster,
" had often grossly resisted the fourth command-
" ment, how he had not fulfilled the wish of his
" parents, that he should give himself to study, but
" had gone his own way : his wounds did not pain

" him, only his sins. I directed him to Christ, who
" had borne the sins of us all, and who did not
" thrust away the lost son when he humbly and
" penitently asked to be pardoned. At last I suc-
" ceeded in calming him: he took hold of my hand
" firmly, and begged me not to leave him. Afterwards
" I visited the hospital which was attended by the
" Sisters of Mercy: they took me from room to room
" with great courtesy, and without displaying any
" offence at my showing forth Christ as the only way
" to find peace of soul and joy of heart." At the
battle of Aschaffenburg, the same field preacher
found an opportunity of taking six Austrians prisoner
without exposing himself to capture by the enemy.
The battle there had been short and decisive, and
the enemy beat a hasty retreat, leaving great numbers of wounded and a large quantity of baggage
upon the road. He had been working hard all the
morning in administering both spiritual and temporal relief, and sat down at last quite exhausted in
the forecourt of a large house belonging to some
nobleman, and there refreshed himself with a glass

of wine, which was handed him by the people of the house, who told him that there were some disguised Austrians in their factory buildings, and that they feared future unpleasantness if they kept them concealed. He went to the place pointed out, and found there six Austrians, whom he challenged to lay down their arms and to follow him to a Prussian troop. They complied without much hesitation, and he delivered them up to an officer whom he met escorting another batch of prisoners. The same chaplain describes a different kind of experience at Uettingen in the following terms: " The flank " march of the Wrangel brigade upon our right " wing had begun; its artillery was in full fire, and " the batteries were also about to open upon our " left wing, when the colonel of the 13th regiment, " who had, in order to reconnoitre, ridden into the " corn-field in front of which the artillery stood, " came back and told me that two artillerymen were " lying in the corn badly wounded, and that they " must be removed at once, in order not to be ex- " posed anew to the fire of the shells. I immediately

" brought the ambulance corps with two litters, and
" hurried them into the field where the men were
" lying. A major of artillery called out to me to
" make haste, as a battery was about to open just
" upon the spot. We were still seeking for the
" wounded men when it was dismounted and began
" to fire. The enemy answered promptly; and
" while we hastened off with the wounded soldiers
" on to the high road behind our battery, right in
" the line of the enemy's fire, the shells flew whizzing
" and exploding about us and over our heads.
" These were indeed anxious moments, as we (in
" spite of the shells) had to move along quite slowly
" with our serious charge. I committed my soul to
" the Lord, and experienced His protecting hand
" held over me."

These extracts from the various diaries of the
spiritual warriors will serve to give the reader some
idea of the real scenes which occur upon the track
even of a victorious army. They form a strange
contrast with the glory of victory. We will only
add one other picture, taken between Rossbrunn and

Helmstadt, before passing to the most trying of all
the chaplain's duties.   Our narrator says: " At
" the edge of a forest I found a young Bavarian
" officer lying much hurt; he had had a ball
" through his body, and one eye appeared quite
" destroyed.   He committed to me his last messages
" for his loved ones, and his last bequests.   I received
" his watch and his pocket-book, promising to for-
" ward them to his relations.   He was suffering from
" thirst, and I gave him a draught of my communion
" wine, for unfortunately my travelling flask was
" broken.   To my joy, his languid eye brightened
" again in a few moments.   His best friend, a Bava-
" rian captain, was lying about two hundred paces
" further on, shot through the legs.   His faithful
" attendant was sitting by him supporting his head,
" and his little dog was licking his wounds.   It was
" the 32nd regiment, mostly composed of Saxons
" and Wupperthalers, which had to bear the heat of
" the fighting in this valley.   Never in the course
" of my life have I longed for water so much as I
" did then, for these wounded men were tormented

" with burning thirst. The ambulance corps was
" unable to attend to so many as quickly as was
" necessary. My small flask of communion wine
" was soon spent; and then I could do no more for
" their bodies, though still able to draw water out
" of the ever-flowing wells of salvation wherewith to
" refresh the souls of these sufferers."

CHAPTER VIII.

IN THE HOSPITALS.

TOWARDS the close of the last chapter, we said that this would be devoted to another and still more arduous part of the chaplain's duties. There is a certain amount of excitement which carries one through the scenes of active warfare, and renders one comparatively indifferent to the miseries and dangers of the field. A regular military hospital has, however, a far different effect upon those who have to spend their days within its walls.

To civilians, the word "hospital" suggests a clean, large building, with hundreds of beds, lofty rooms, wide corridors, and a good supply of all the necessaries of life, sisters to nurse the sick, numerous

surgeons in attendance, members of the order of
St. John going in and out, volunteer sick nurses
helping both bodily and spiritually, and whatever
else that is beautiful in ministry. There may, perhaps, at some period during the war, have been
hospitals answering to this description; but how
long were they likely to last, when cases of the
worst description were brought in so rapidly that it
was difficult to furnish anything more than tolerable
repose? Take, as a specimen, the large hospital
which was established in the school-house of Königinhof, as it appeared a few days after the battle.
You ascended the steps, and passed through the
corridors, which were covered with straw and filth,
while a pestilential smell arose from the neighbouring apartments. The school-rooms had their benches
piled up on one side, while, on the other, lay the
wounded in a long row upon a little straw, their
cloaks forming their only covering. In the largest
room were some of the Austrian officers who had
been brought in; they had mattrasses, but there
was not the trace of a bedstead. It must be ac-

knowledged, however, that, in consequence especially
of the unwearying attention of the Knights of St.
John, some degree of order was generally brought
about; though it was long before the charitable
contributions of the people at home found their way
here; and those smaller hospitals which were lying
much out of the way never received any benefit
therefrom. Even as late as the 15th July the hospital of Königinhof could not accommodate the
necessary number, and many had to be content with
a lodging in close and uncomfortable quarters,
where a pestiferous smell often prevailed. Most of
the wounded were still lying upon the floor, on
bundles of straw and mattrasses, and only scantily
supplied with pillows and coverlets. Notwithstanding this, all praise is due to the members of the order
of St. John, the deacons and deaconesses, grey sisters,
surgeons, and sick nurses, who did their utmost, and
who had generally large stores of comforts at their
disposal.

. Of all the horrible scenes of utter misery, none,
however, could equal the cholera hospitals, which had

subsequently to be established at all the principal places on the line of march. These were absolutely beyond description. Let us, however, accompany an eye-witness to the principal hospital at the castle of L——. "The inspector did not dare to show us " through the sick chambers of the various floors, as " he was already suffering from colic, and he counselled " us to avoid the worst. We did not allow ourselves " to be dissuaded, but went from one room to another. " The frightful condition in which we found the " patients cannot be described; the cholera and " typhus patients lay with glazed eyes, staring va- " cantly at us; they had no covering over them except " their soldiers' cloaks, their legs were bare, and " some were lying on straw without any sacking; " they had no one to attend on them, and were " groaning aloud and talking incoherently, in the " midst of filth and dirt, without even a nurse or " attendant of any kind to cleanse the rooms. The " number of invalids in the castle amounted to " ninety-four; during the preceding night eleven " of them had died, and fresh waggons were con-

" tinually arriving, bringing those who were dying
" or extremely ill, while some had actually died
" upon the way. The burial of the dead was simply
" impossible; the bodies were heaped up in two great
" sheds, and infected the air. The hospital was
" wanting in all the principal requisites, in ban-
" dages, woollen cloths, red wine, biscuits, &c., for in
" these wretched places such things were not to be
" had. We turned away with horror, quite in doubt
" where to begin and where to end. We entered a
" second large hospital in the same place, which the
" pestilence had quickly filled. On the road to it we
" met four soldiers carrying a typhus patient only
" half clothed; in his delirium he had made his escape
" during the night, and had only just been caught.
" The next hospital was, if possible, in a worse con-
" dition; the man who had kept watch during the
" night previous, said that he found one man sit-
" ting dead upon a water-closet, another lying dead
" across the threshold of a large ward, and a third
" fell into his arms and died. At another place,
" where the arrangements were reported to be

" tolerably complete, the hospital was established on
" the stone floor of a large church, round the high
" roof of which the groans and moans of the wounded
" echoed horribly. The invalids begged for drink
" in the most piteous tones; but there was no red
" wine to be had, and they were not allowed to
" touch the water. When the clergyman arrived
" at Brünn who was to have charge of the first
" cholera hospital, which was established there on
" the Spielberg, he found already two hundred and
" forty-nine cholera patients, with only one staff
" surgeon, one field deacon, and two almost useless
" attendants. There was no water, no fire, no rags,
" not even bundles of straw or mattrasses."

This is no exceptional picture; most of the chaplains had to witness similar scenes at first; and
though the arrangements became subsequently more
complete, the demand for their services increased, so
that those who did hospital duty had to exercise
no small amount of self-sacrifice.

The rapidity of the military movements, and the
subsequent outbreak of cholera, threw most unex-

pected difficulties in the way of the chaplains, for which they were by no means prepared. The consequence was, that during the earlier period of the campaign, and in Moravia, where the cholera was worst, there was a most lamentable deficiency of spiritual agency. It was the combination of these circumstances which called forth the army of volunteers, which has been referred to in our first article; but then the question arose how best to utilize this volunteer force. Those who thus came forward to help were not under the strict control of the regular chaplains; and while anxious to be useful, they had still their own ideas as to where to go, and what kind of service they should perform. The consequence was that they accumulated in places which were convenient of access, and often experienced the unpleasant rebuff that they were not wanted; while the hospitals lying in places remote from the high roads were left utterly destitute. The spots, indeed, where their presence was most wanted were utterly unknown to them: places like Landeshut, Trautenau, Gorlitz, and Reichenberg, in Bohemia, and the head-quarters in Moravia at Brünn, were filled with applicants, while within a few miles either to the right or left were hospitals where their assistance would have been most welcome. It is uncertain how long this state of affairs might have lasted; but, fortunately, Von Hengstenberg, the court chaplain, visited the principal hospitals in Northern Bohemia, at the request of the Chaplain-General of the Forces; and almost simultaneously Dr. Erdmann, the General Superintendent of the Province of Silesia, proceeded to the frontier to regulate the supplies within his province. Dr. Erdmann made some important suggestions, which were carried out to a considerable extent on the occasion in question, but which may perhaps have more than a passing interest. His recommendation was that the large military hospitals within the theatre of war should constitute a special military diocese under the control of an inspector: for this purpose a superior military chaplain should be told off, if one can be spared, or, if not, a divisional chaplain or any other who has authority and a faculty for organization.

He should be thoroughly equipped with a carriage and three horses, to enable him freely to pass through all parts of his diocese, and to convey to his sphere of action any brother minister who may be sent to him.

At their joint recommendations, Pastor Weikert was entrusted by the Chaplain-General of the Forces with the inspectorship of the hospitals in Bohemia; and this appointment proved a very great blessing, not only to the ministers themselves, but to the people under their charge. These were all under his personal superintendence, and before passing to other districts let us take a look at the establishments which formed his temporary episcopate.

His head-quarters were established at Königinhof, because that was the most central and important point. It was not only the scene of a great battle, but was immediately surrounded by the memorable fields of Trautenau, Skalitz, Gitschin, and Königgrätz, while, at the same time, the railways communicating with Prussia converged upon this point, so that it was one of the most busy centres of the whole cam-

paign. When he commenced his duties, on the
16th of July, all the houses, the market-place, the
streets, and covered alleys of the town, were no
longer crowded with the wounded and the dying, as
was the case for a few days after the battle, but the
white banners were still floating over twenty-three
establishments. The chief hospital was the medical
school. The great building belonging to the upper
city school, and the girls' school, had every wing
and floor filled with wounded soldiers, to the number
of about three hundred. Next in importance were
Mann's Gardens, in which were two large tents, while
the saloon was converted into a chapel; then the
Black Eagle Hotel, in the great hall of which an
altar was erected for the Roman Catholic service;
the deanery, the machine and workrooms of the
large spinning-mill, in the dwelling-house attached
to which Prince Anthony of Hohenzollern lay and
died,—all were filled with wounded soldiers. In the
railway station even, ten tents were put up for their
reception, besides one room which was set apart for
officers. The town hospital was reserved exclusively

for cases of cholera and typhus. Such was the place
where Pastor Weikert commenced his labours. He
was not, however, without able assistants, and some of
these had prevented his arrival. The regimental
surgeon, Dr. von Schleinitz, had a large store of
hospital necessaries at the railway depôt, which he
judiciously distributed, in which he was greatly aided
by Madame von Seydlitz, who presided over the
culinary department, and so added greatly to the
comfort of the sufferers. Several of the regimental
chaplains had stopped a day or two on their onward
march, in order to visit and comfort the wounded and
dying, and to administer the Lord's Supper to such as
desired it; but when Weikert entered upon his new
duties he had only one permanent assistant here, a
missionary from Breslau. The hospitals of Königinhof alone were more than one clergyman could
attend to; and as he had diocesan duties also, it was
necessary that he should find some one to relieve
him of a great portion of the former. He found a
most valuable assistant in the person of Dr. Bertheau,
a theological candidate, who had been sent to him as

a field deacon. He laboured there indefatigably for nearly four weeks, visiting the patients regularly, speaking words of consolation to the sick, reading and praying with them, holding public prayer-meetings, writing letters for them to their relations, distributing the Scriptures, and, in short, showing himself in every way to be a sympathetic and untiring friend.

It would weary the reader were we to notice all the places under Weikert's episcopal care. At Arnau there were only about forty wounded soldiers, and as a regular chaplain could not be spared for so small a number, he arranged that the Lutheran pastor of a neighbouring village should attend to them and supply the men with Testaments: this clergyman had been suspected at the commencement of the war of being a spy and a secret friend to the Prussians, and his life had been repeatedly threatened by his own countrymen in consequence.

A large manufactory at Reddendorf had been turned into a hospital, and it contained about fifty patients; only three of them, however, were Prus-

sians, and the surgical staff was exclusively Austrian.
The medical men had supplied them with unsuitable books, and playing-cards! and the poor Prussians were greatly rejoiced to receive a visit from
a Protestant clergyman.

The cloister of Kukus, charmingly situated on
the Elbe, sheltered about sixty invalids. The sick-
room, a small high-vaulted church with an altar,
was remarkable for the beauty of its wood carving.
The bedsteads, which belonged to the previous cen-
tury, were highly ornamented, and in themselves
quite worth a visit. The outer side of each bed
bore a biblical quotation, which furnished a suitable
sermon for its wounded occupant.

The whole town of Horsitz formed one great
hospital. Not only were many private houses occupied by the wounded, but they were also lying in
the streets, the market-place, manufactory, the
school-house, theatre, mining-house, and palace. Of
the five hundred or so wounded men who were left
here about seventy were Prussians, who were attended by two deacons and a Protestant deaconess.

The senior deacon held a public service every Sunday in the Roman Catholic church for the military garrison; and every Prussian invalid in the town had his New Testament, his Thomas à Kempis, and other good books, and, what is more, had read them. About five English miles to the south-east is the Palace of Cerekwice, where there were at first from three hundred to four hundred wounded soldiers, amongst whom the Prussians numbered eighty at most, the others being almost exclusively Roman Catholics, and few of them even speaking German. The Sisters of the order of St. Borromeo attended the sick with most self-sacrificing love, even reading Protestant books to the Prussian soldiers; while the Knights of St. John assisted the chaplain in his spiritual charge. The hospitals of Horennowes and Maslowed were also well cared for, as they enjoyed the advantage of having four deaconesses, whose beautiful singing in the public services held by the chaplain afforded much pleasure to the sufferers. In some places, however, they were not so fortunate: at Vsestar, for instance, the Romish priest

took away from the soldiers the Scriptures given
them by Pastor Delius.   On the latter remonstrating
with him, he remarked: " The Scriptures you dis-
" tribute defend duelling; and there is no need for
" the Bible to be read by sick men."   Nechanitz
contained some four hundred wounded, of whom
about half were Protestants.   Bible and prayer
meetings were held here daily, in which the chaplain was much encouraged by the officers, one of
whom openly acknowledged that it was upon his
sick bed that he first learnt to believe.

Pardubitz was an important medical station
throughout the campaign, less for the wounded
than for those who were overtaken with cholera,
fever, and other complaints.   There were generally
from three hundred to four hundred sick in the various
hospitals of the town, the number being kept up by
those left behind from the different regiments as
they passed through.   In consequence of his flock
constantly changing, the chaplain would not have
had a sufficient supply of Testaments and hymn-
books, had he not established the rule that none

should take the books away with them on their recovery unless they learnt some verses of the Psalms
or hymns. He was gratified to see whole rooms
full of learners, and fostered the hope that the books
thus earned would be duly prized, and that what
was learnt would also bear more fruit than what
was merely read. A soldier who scarcely knew more
than his letters spelt through many verses in succession, and imprinted them on his memory with
great labour, in order to possess himself of a book.
As the burial of those who died from cholera had
to take place quickly, Pastor Willich merely offered
up a prayer on such occasions, and then gave the
benediction. On Sundays he held Divine service
with the troops in a Roman Catholic church,
Fliedner, a theological student, leading the singing,
and a Roman Catholic teacher playing the organ.

Gitschin was a point of much importance throughout the war. All the large buildings in the town
were converted into hospitals, and they were clean
and well attended. Magnus, the principal chaplain
here, had a great work before him, and had, too, the

joy of seeing much blessing attend his labours. Not only did about ten die from their wounds each day, but the cholera raged throughout the town, carrying off about twenty of the townspeople daily. Five of the attendants at the hospitals, one surgeon, and one Alexian brother, also died of the same disease. The chaplain received much kindness from all sections of the community, dwelling in the house of the Roman Catholic dean, and preaching on Sundays in the Roman Catholic church. He was also much assisted by the sisters of Kaiserswerth, and a young lady, who attended the cholera hospital, and from Von Werder, one of the Knights of St. John, who supplied bodily comforts with liberal hand. A letter written by one of the soldiers to his relations at home will serve to show with what zeal both the temporal and spiritual concerns of the wounded were cared for. It ran thus :—

" MY BELOVED PARENTS, BROTHERS AND SISTERS,

" Your telegraphic despatch is the first sign " of life that I have received from you. None of the

" letters which you have written have ever reached
" me. It was indeed a pleasure to receive, at last,
" two words from home. Dear parents, you need not
" write again, as I am not likely to get your letters
" for four weeks, if at all, and I know now that you
" are all well. I will gladly send you another letter,
" if possible, that you may learn how it fares with
" me. I am very much better already,—I have
" scarcely any pain now. God will, perhaps, out of His
" great grace and mercy, restore me to full vigour
" again. I have now all I can desire : a bed, two
" coverlets, good sugar, two cups of chocolate daily,
" as well as bouillon, ham, plums, if I wish them, and
" milk every afternoon, so that I do not want any-
" thing more ; wine, beer, and cigars, which the
" others have, I do not grudge, as I dare not enjoy
" them. Again I add, dear parents, I am doing
" well. I live happily with my dear Lord God now.
" Once it was going very badly with me, and I
" thought that my end was near. Then the Lord
" sent me His servant, who administered the Lord's
" Supper to me, and directed me to Christ. For some

" days I have been much better in body and soul.
" Several ministers come here now, and bring us all
" heavenly consolation. The court preacher, Von
" Hengstenberg, has been here. Herr Von Oertzen,
" the dear kind man who wrote to you in my name,
" has sent me a beautiful New Testament. Yester-
" day a good gentleman came here who brought us
" many interesting books; then he comforted us,
" read a Psalm aloud, prayed, and gave the benedic-
" diction. Ah! dear parents, these are blessed hours.
" My dear neighbour Mitzlaff, who has lost a foot,
" constantly reads to me, and I try to console him
" when he suffers severe pain. His foot is healing
" well. I am thankful to say we are one in heart and
" soul. We thank the members of the order of St
" John, after God, for being so well off, for they have
" laboured most arduously and efficiently. There are
" now six sisters from Trier amongst us, who tend to
" our needs with Christian love and patience. If I
" get well again, dear parents, you will find me quite
" a different man; for up to this time I have only
" been a miserable servant of sin; but God's grace

" is all-sufficient. Pray God earnestly and constantly
" for me. May you keep well. Kisses to all dear
" ones.

" Your

" HENRY."

The hospital at Sobotka, where there were about
sixty invalids, was superintended by Pastor Lohmann,
who held morning and evening prayer daily with
them, and who preached on Sundays in the Roman
Catholic church, the priest himself being one of his
hearers, who even attended one celebration of the
Lord's Supper. Whenever he had to officiate at a
funeral, he went through the full service, the im-
pressiveness of which was evidently felt by the
Roman Catholics, who used to be present in numbers
on those occasions.

In the four hospitals of Reichenberg there were
on an average from two hundred to three hundred wounded, of whom about one-fourth were
Protestants. Brother Kleinschmidt, a minister of
the United Brethren, had charge of them, and he
was assisted by a couple of deacons. Besides minis-

tering to the men individually as they lay upon
their sick beds, he dispensed the Lord's Supper to
many, held the funeral services over the graves of
those who died, and conducted a Bible study in one
of the hospitals every Sunday afternoon. Finding a
number of Hungarians there who did not understand
German, he suggested the propriety of procuring
the services of some Bohemian minister who knew
their language; but though his plan received the
approval of the Government, he was unable to carry
it out, as none of the Protestant ministers in that
part of Bohemia would venture to go hand in hand
with their Prussian brethren. At Prague, however,
a much better feeling existed, and for some time the
large hospitals at the capital were principally tended
by the resident Protestant ministers; but on the return of a large portion of the troops to Prague, the
number of sick increased to such an extent that an
addition to the spiritual agency was absolutely
necessary; two permanent hospital chaplains were
accordingly sent, in addition to those who were attached to the regiments quartered there; and their

energies were taxed to the utmost in attending to the five large hospitals at Prague, which were constantly full of patients.

We must now take leave of Bohemia, and turn to Moravia, where some fnew experiences will meet us. The corps d'armée which we shall now accompany did not go through so much fighting, but fell in with a much more formidable enemy than the Austrians —the cholera. Brünn, the capital, was appointed head-quarters of the hospital service ; indeed the whole city might be considered one great hospital, but some of the smaller towns in Moravia were even in a much worse condition. The city itself is beautifully situated at the foot of the Spielberg; and its numerous towers and church spires suggested pleasing associations to the soldiers, who looked forward to a comfortable resting-place after their long and wearisome marches. How miserably were their hopes disappointed! The name of Brünn will ever suggest to those who visited it at this time a scene of indescribable wretchedness, rather than that of a picturesque old city. As early as the end of

M

July it contained fourteen hospitals, with fifteen
hundred inmates, and this number greatly increased
in the month of August. To a very large proportion
of these Brünn became the last resting-place. In
addition to the chaplains who were attached to the
troops on the march, and which were quartered here
for longer or shorter periods, there was a very large
staff of hospital chaplains, mostly volunteers, all of
whom were most courteously entertained by the
resident Protestant ministers, Schur and Trauten-
berger, in whose houses they used to enjoy brotherly
communion and spiritual refreshment, after the toils
of the day were over. Circumstances which could
not be foreseen tended to cause a comparative accu-
mulation of ministers at this spot, to the disadvantage
of many other places, where their services were even
more urgently needed. Being the capital, they naturally made for that point, and finding a large sphere
of usefulness open to them, they did not care to
inquire further; moreover, there was no general
superintendent appointed for the Moravian hospitals,
as was the case in Bohemia, because the agreement

for an armistice was made at the end of July, and
every one regarded the war as virtually at an end,
while it was almost simultaneously with this, that the
numerous hospitals sprung into existence in consequence of the violent outburst of cholera. The short
time that the occupation of Moravia lasted, was, however, quite sufficient to show how important it is to
provide beforehand for all contingencies. Had there
been a superior chaplain appointed at the first entry
of the army into Moravia, assistance would have been
quickly sent from Brünn to some of the wretched
places which we must now describe.

Amongst these Lundenburg occupied a prominent
rank. In point of numbers of cholera patients it was
only second to Brünn itself, while the general
unhealthiness of the town, which is situated in a
swamp, added to the wretchedness; and the desolate
railway station, through which the wind always
whistled, and the dirty houses, mostly deserted of
their proper inhabitants, completed the picture of
misery and woe. Nevertheless, in consequence of
being situated at the junction of the Brünn and

Olmütz railways, it was particularly important as a military station. From hence the army of Prince Frederick Charles had to take its eastern course towards the Carpathians, near Presburg; and, subsequently, when the railway was again rendered practicable, it was the spot fixed upon for victualling the army, which radiated from thence to the Carpathian and Moravian mountains. It was, therefore, unavoidable that those who were once overtaken by disease should be gathered together in large numbers at Lundenburg. On hearing that spiritual help was needed, Pastor Trogisch proceeded thither from Brünn, and found about three hundred cholera and typhus patients in the palace, a house, and a manufactory, the greater part of whom were in an apparently helpless condition. Neither the staff of attendants nor the hospital supplies could keep pace with the rapid increase of invalids, although Pastor Eichler, who accompanied fourteen deacons to the seat of war, sent nine of them back to Lundenburg. The cholera also raged throughout the civil community, so that the bells of the priests who were on their way to the sick tinkled incessantly. But no sooner had their necessitous state become known, than the knightly order of the Samaritans made their appearance, under Count Theodore Von Stolberg, who, with most devoted zeal, bestowed his welcome gifts on the suffering men, supplying them with coverlets, pillows, mattrasses, and red wine. In ministering spiritually to these invalids, time was even more precious than with the wounded, if they were to hear a word of comfort and warning, or to receive the sacrament of the Lord's Supper. In two days the latter was administered to seventy in preparation for death. " The misery," writes Pastor Trogisch in his report, " was overwhelming. The awful scenes almost de-" prived me of power. It was grievous for the men " to die without their sighs and complaints being " heard; and how much harder the struggle with " pestilential disease in the hospital, than death " upon the field of honour! So at least it appears, " and so it was said to be. Death indeed reaped his " harvest." As a specimen, and by no means an unfavourable one, we may take the register of deaths for four days: on the 2nd August, 22; on the 3rd, 20; on the 4th and 5th, 16 each day. Some deaconesses subsequently came, as well as Roman Catholic brethren from Prague; two theological students also discharged the duties of deacons. All laboured together in harmony, under the leadership of the noble Count Stolberg, so that the heaviest part of the work was soon overcome, and they were even able to render some assistance to the outlying hospitals towards Presburg. With the help of the royal Prussian commandant, they, moreover, secured a small chapel, in which public service was held on Sundays to strengthen the ministers for the labours of the coming week.

Almost every place on the road from Brünn to Nicolsburg was converted into a hospital—Kostel, the stately abbey of Raigern, Pohrlitz, and others which we cannot stop to enumerate. Even Nicolsburg itself, the royal head-quarters, which for several weeks became the most important spot in all Europe, did not escape the ravages of the cholera: 136 fresh mounds in the military cemetery,

which was consecrated on the occasion, tell with
what effect the plague swept over this immediate
neighbourhood. At Wilffersdorf, Chaplain Rogge,
with the rest of the staff of the 1st division of
Foot Guards, took up his quarters during the
armistice at the castle of Prince Lichtenstein, the
palace being appropriated to the commander of the
division. " But," he says, " it had to be given up
" to the dismal guest who for some days had dogged
" our steps; and when we appeared at the dinner-
" table in the quarters of our general, who had to
" be satisfied in consequence with some of the offices
" immediately adjoining, the unpleasant inscription
" over the door, ' Cholera Hospital,' served as a
" *memento mori* for the more earnest, and a warn-
" ing against errors of diet at the least, for the most
" frivolous. During our week's stay I had special
" opportunities of learning by direct evidence many
" details as to the horrors of the pestilence; and
" I cannot deny that it cost me an effort at first to
" shake the hand of a cholera patient, when he
" stretched it forth to me in his joy at seeing me

" again. I did not hesitate afterwards in doing so
" with those who were even extremely ill. During
" these days I felt how much harder and more
" wearisome is the work in cholera hospitals, than at
" the dressing places of the wounded. With the
" latter one could be cheerful, for it was always
" encouraging to observe the resignation with which
" the soldiers bore their pain, and how attentively
" they listened to the chaplain while telling them
" the result of the battle in which they had received
" their wounds, and how the very consciousness of
" having received them in the immediate exercise of
" their calling and in the discharge of their duty, sus-
" tained them throughout. How different it was in
" the cholera hospitals! the common complaint was,
" ' Oh! that after enduring all the hardships, and
" ' after having been spared in all the battles, I
" ' should perish so miserably here!' The defiant and
" the fainthearted both laid their complaints against
" the dealings of Providence, and showed much less
" disposition to submit to the imposed cross, and to
" the idea of death. And then to observe the

" horrible pains in all their limbs! It went through
" bone and marrow when a cholera patient cried out
" because of the fearful cramps in his thighs and
" calves, and tried the attendants much more than
" when a wounded man gave audible expression to
" his sufferings. The number of those who sank
" into complete unconsciousness was very great.
" The doctors and attendants, spending day and
" night in pestiferous or draughty rooms, had to
" undergo a fearful amount of labour; and many of
" them remarked that they needed to brace up all
" their powers in order to keep themselves up to the
" mark, as they needed more vigour in such places
" than at the dressing places in the midst of and
" under the shells of the enemy." At this hospital
both a surgeon and a dispenser were attacked by
cholera; and though the former happily recovered,
the latter became a martyr to his unhealthy
calling.

Not far distant lies Mistelbach, with its stately
cloister dedicated to St. Barnabas, which was converted into a hospital. Pastor Wedepohl took up

his quarters within the sacred retreat, whilst the brigade to which he was attached was stationed in the village; and he devoted himself with the greatest zeal to the sick and dying, receiving at the same time much friendly assistance from the monks. The latter, however, had an eye to more worldly amusements also, and expressed themselves much pleased with the Prussian officers, who used to come and drink coffee and play at bowls with them under the beautiful avenues of lime trees. Whether they had been blamed for their associating with Protestants does not appear, but a story went the round of the Vienna papers, complaining of the barbarity of the Prussians, who had worried the monks of Mistelbach!

CHAPTER IX.

HOSPITAL DUTIES.

THE south-western part of Germany, which was occupied by the Army of the Maine, furnished experiences peculiar to itself; and the first hospital which commands our attention is that of Kissingen. The great Kursaal, with its beautiful colonnades, surrounding the springs and medicinal waters, which are so familiar to most travellers, resembled in the summer in question the pool of Bethesda. Instead of the world of fashion who usually take their pleasure in the long colonnades, there was a long row of wounded soldiers lying on their bags of straw upon the ground, who even passed their nights out there during the warm weather which immediately suc-

ceeded the battle.   Instead of the dance music with
which the great hall usually resounds, there were
heard groans, cries of pain, and the death-rattle.
But He who said to the man who had been sick for
thirty-eight years, " Wilt thou be made whole ?" and
who told him to take up his bed and walk, was also
here in spirit.   The Kissingen people mutually
outvied one another in the self-denial with which
they cared for both the South German and Prussian
wounded; their best rooms and beds were at their
service; and as the town is laid out for the reception
of invalids and bathers, there were such an amount
of accommodation and variety of conveniences for
the sick as were furnished by few other places.
They were also efficiently supplied with spiritual
comfort, not only by the regular chaplains accompanying the army, but also by Superintendent
Dürselen, who was sent there by the Elberfeld
Committee.

At Hammelsberg there were about one hundred
and twenty wounded in hospital, and amongst them
General Schachtmeyer, who, as he lay upon his couch,

cheerfully acknowledged how greatly God had protected him, showing that five balls had passed through
his coat without hurting him. Both these places,
however, were so crowded—a good part of the latter
having been burnt down—that a number of the
wounded were sent to the charming bathing-place
Brückenau, where they received the best attention,
both bodily and spiritually, and were amply supplied
with Testaments and Prayer-books. Several severe
engagements took place in this neighbourhood, so that
almost every village had its hospital. At Aschaffenburg there were six, which sheltered a large number
of wounded Prussians as well as many hundreds of
Austrians and Hessians. Tauberbischofsheim was
another place of importance in this respect, the
division Goeben having suffered very severely at this
spot; and Pastor Dietz (who was also one of the
delegates from Elberfeld) remained here for six weeks,
holding daily morning and evening prayer with the
wounded, as well as regular services on Sundays
for the military and the civilians.

In this part of Germany there was no one set

apart to regulate the supply of chaplains at the different hospitals; and those who volunteered their services had to find for themselves their respective spheres of labour. Pastor Niessmann had thus been sent by the Elberfeld Committee to Frankfort, and he did not know which way to direct his steps. On the 26th July he was standing in front of his hotel, when he was accosted by a student who was serving as deacon in the Army of the Maine, and who told him that an important battle had just taken place at Uettingen, and that a military train, with surgeons and hospital supplies, would leave in the evening for the battle-field. He regarded this as a call from God, and joyfully embraced the opportunity. On arriving at his sphere of labour, he found white flags floating over numbers of the houses, under the protection of which he found five hundred and sixty wounded men. This was almost more than he could attend to; but after the first pressure of work was over, he found time to visit also the neighbouring towns of Remlingen, Rossbrunn, and Mädelhofen.

A painful interest attaches to Remlingen as the

only spot hallowed by the death of a military chaplain during this brief war. We refer to Superior Chaplain Koch, who was snatched away by cholera from an active sphere, just at a time when he appeared to be most needed. The following narrative is in the words of a brother in office, who was near him during the closing hours of his life, and who followed him to his last resting-place in the cemetery of Remlingen : " I first met him on the " 30th of July in Remlingen, where he (appointed to " the superior chaplaincy of the Army of the Maine, " and ordered into the head-quarters) had remained " with the staff of the Division Fliess, and had " striven in some measure to bring order out of the " confusion which prevailed in the hospitals lying " around. When I looked into his friendly face " and kindly eyes, out of which beamed a heart full " of love and self-denial, I realized in him one of " those people to whom you feel irresistibly drawn, " and who inspires a mutual confidence, if only the " same faith rules both spirits. At the battle of " Uettingen he had given clear proof of his self-

" denying love, riding on horseback in the midst of
" the battle to where the wounded were lying in
" greatest number, utterly regardless of the danger
" to his own life.   After he had conferred with the
" ministers in Uettingen as to the best arrangements
" that could be made in the hospitals, he held a
" public service at Remlingen at seven o'clock in
" the evening, when he preached from Philippians
" iv. 7.   He always spoke earnestly; but many of
" his hearers have told me since that he never
" preached more powerfully than on this occasion.
" He referred to the peace, and the return home
" to the fatherland, which was then in prospect,
" urging that it might lead to the peace of God,
" which is higher and more enduring, and directing
" his hearers to the true heavenly home.   When at
" the church he was much heated, and complained of
" being unwell; but next morning I met him in Uet-
" tingen as lively and vigorous as usual.   He visited
" wounded officers at that place, and then returned
" to Remlingen.   On Wednesday, the 1st of August,
" I went into his quarters, which consisted of a

" large room in a peasant's house, which he occupied
" in common with his Roman Catholic colleague. I
" wished to ask him which hospital I should best
" visit. I found him hoarse, and lying in bed, but
" certainly not smitten at that time with the fell
" disease. His first words were, 'Do not hurry
" ' away, but remain near at hand till I am well
" ' again; I have work enough for you here.' So I
" remained, and passed as much time as I could
" spare at his couch. Every time we met we
" opened our hearts more and more to one another.
" We constantly realized the words of the apostle,
" ' As unknown and yet well known.' To give an
" instance of this, he spoke of his happiness in
" his office of military chaplain, and thankfully
" recalled the various experiences of his life. He
" referred with great affection to his Roman Catholic
" colleague. Then he reflected upon his home life,
" how fortunate he was to possess an only daughter,
" who had written him a letter a few days previously.
" When I entered his room on the 2nd of August,
" I found the dear pastor much depressed, and

N

" suffering from all the symptoms of cholera. His
" salutation to me was, 'Dear brother, I have had a
" ' very bad night.' This was his only complaint,
" while his restlessness, and the coldness of his
" hands and feet, told of the increase of the disease.
" He still, however, cherished the hope of recovery.
" At midday Field Deacon Benemann came to attend
" him, and he would not, therefore, let me stay. As
" I was leaving the room, he called me to his side,
" folded his hands, and commenced the hymn,
" ' Though our sin is great,'—' Pray with me.' We
" repeated the precious verse together, and then
" I went to my own quarters at the house of the
" hospitable Protestant clergyman Matthäus. On
" the following morning I was aroused early with
" the tidings that he was very ill; and as I was
" hastening to see him, faithful Benemann called to
" me from outside the door, 'Koch is dead.' He
" had tossed about up to one o'clock in the morning
" with increasing delirium, and in the brief intervals
" of composure had repeated with Benemann the
" 103rd Psalm ; then he grew calmer and slept, while

" the deacon sat beside his bed, and, having covered
" his patient up warmly, he also went to sleep.
" When he awoke, he rejoiced to think that Koch
" still slept so quietly, but quickly discovered that
" he was dead. By seven o'clock his body was taken
" to the dead-house. I never before understood, as
" I did then, our Lord's words, 'Our friend Lazarus
" ' sleepeth.' Such blessed peace was reflected in
" his countenance. As the staff of the division of
" General Fliess, who wished to pay the last honours
" to the deceased, was to march out next morning,
" our sleeping friend was buried that same evening
" at six o'clock, in the cemetery of Remlingen. His
" grave was the first beside which I stood in my
" capacity as field preacher. A large proportion
" of the inhabitants accompanied us to his last rest-
" ing-place, where I delivered the funeral address
" from the words in 1 John iii. 16, 'Hereby perceive
" ' we the love of God, because He laid down His
" ' life for us; and we ought to lay down our lives
" ' for the brethren.' Pastor Matthäus, who, with .
" the Roman Catholic field chaplain, and a Roman

" Catholic brother from the neighbouring village, took
" part in the ceremony, offered up prayer with deep
" emotion and manifest sympathy, and pronounced
" the benediction. Whenever I conversed with
" officers and soldiers who had known the deceased,
" I found the truth of the word he declared had not
" been without fruit. The memory of the righteous
" is blessed; and I have since experienced anew the
" love that all had for him. He had made many
" friends during the Schleswig campaign, and since
" then as divisional chaplain in Schleswig. His
" former flock in Sommerfeld also held him in friendly
" and thankful remembrance."

We cannot dwell longer on the hospitals of this
part of Germany, except to mention that there were
many others at Helmstädt, Würzburg, Homburg,
Wiesbaden, &c., besides Frankfort, which was naturally selected for the central establishment. Most of
the sick who could be removed were brought here.
By the 22nd of July there were five large hospitals,
with over one thousand wounded, while the number
was subsequently largely increased by cholera and

typhus patients. At first Pastor Krummacher, of Elberfeld, had the entire spiritual charge; but assistance soon arrived from various quarters, so that ultimately there was no lack, though the want of proper organization was very much felt.

The hospitals in Saxony do not require much notice, though Dresden naturally formed an important station, as there was a military camp there, and generally from one thousand seven hundred to one thousand eight hundred sick and wounded, including Austrians and Saxons. The chaplain who was attached to the First Reserve Corps, which was stationed here, suggested that the resident clergy should attend to the sick, and they readily accepted the proposition, dividing the city into so many wards. They showed equal attention to the Prussians as to their own countrymen; but the work so increased upon their hands that it was found necessary to appoint special hospital chaplains. They were assisted in their spiritual duties in the kindest and most efficient manner by the deaconesses who laboured in the hospitals. They attended to the

burial of the dead, in company with the Roman
Catholic fathers, so that the officers were each
blessed by the clergyman of their own confession;
while the soldiers, who were always buried collec-
tively with military honours, in numbers of about
six at a time, were blessed in turn by the father and
the Protestant minister.   A separation of confessions
was never recognised here, any more than elsewhere,
on such occasions.

Having now referred briefly to the most important
of the hospitals which were established during this
short but decisive campaign, a few general remarks
must be made before passing on to the consideration
of the last sad duty which devolved upon the chaplains.

Altogether there were forty-one ministers employed in the hospitals across the Prussian frontier,
who were supported by voluntary offerings, in addition to all those who were officially connected with
the army : of these no less than twenty-eight were
in Bohemia.   Considering that those of the Prussian
wounded who could be removed were sent home as

soon as possible, it may truly be said that they were
not left without the consolations of the Gospel, even
though the pressure of events and the rapid succession of skirmishes and battles rendered it sometimes impossible to attend to them as soon as might
be wished.

The hospital chaplains found it desirable to adopt
a similar policy to that which has already been
described as generally in use at the dressing places
of the wounded, and offered their services in all
descriptions of ministry, especially in conveying
information to the relatives of the invalids as to
their lot. Many of the hospital preachers and
deacons wrote hundreds of such letters, for which
both the senders and the recipients were heartily
grateful. It was easy enough to write, when the
letter was to convey information of only a slight
wound, and one could add that the patient himself
would write soon ; it was very difficult, however,
when, in all truth, they had to say, " your son,
" your husband, lies mortally wounded," and still
more perplexing when the patient himself begged

them "not to make it out so very bad." On the other hand, they had sometimes most happy experiences to relate as to the spiritual state of those who had passed away. Many curious letters of thanks were received by the chaplains, of which the following, from a poor man in Poland, may serve as a specimen:

" Wazejewo, 8th August.

" DEAR MR. D——,

" Accept my hearty thanks for your goodness,
" it was very kind of you to write me such a comfort-
" ing letter respecting my son Frederick, although
" very painful to his mother and myself to receive;
" nevertheless, we believe that God does all things
" well. Pray do not give up caring for my son.
" Although we can only send you one thaler (3s.)
" to help him just now, we will exert ourselves to
" the utmost, and when we receive your answer we
" will endeavour to send more money. Kind Mr.
" D——, we beg you to be good enough to write us
" an answer as quickly as possible, and let us know
" how our son progresses, whether he is likely to

" be cured, or whether he is already in the church-
" yard. I, my wife, and children, send you greet-
" ings.

" J. K——."

Writing letters naturally made the chaplains
inquire after the homes and household affairs of
the married men, and of the parents of the young
and single men; they gained information as to the
ministers who had confirmed them, and the invalids
were pleased to find them known. The manner in
which the men answered showed at once whether
they were advanced Christians, or had up to that
time been strangers to the Lord and His word ; and
it needed but little acquaintance with pastoral
duties to adapt one's remarks to their varied circumstances.

Many pleasing experiences encouraged the ministers in their arduous labours, while the calmness with
which the soldiers bore pain greatly added to the
comfort of those who ministered to them. It was
frequently remarked that the Austrians, and especially those belonging to the Sclavic races, con-

trasted very unfavourably in this respect with the Prussians. An instance or two of patient endurance may suffice. A Westphalian in the 55th Regiment of Fusiliers stormed the Tauberbrück at Bischof-sheim, with only twenty comrades; a ball penetrated the upper part of his right arm, which split the bone, so that his weapon fell out of his hand; he was taken to the hospital at Bruckenau, and when the chaplain essayed to comfort him, he said, with a bright smile, "Do not think I regret my wound, "pastor, I received it in the service of my beloved "king." He showed, too, that he understood how, not only to suffer joyfully, but also to die cheerfully, when the surgeons decided against amputating his arm, as his strength had failed beyond recovery. General Superintendent Erdmann also met a badly-wounded Westphalian, when making his circuit, and exhorted him to display the same Christian boldness on the bed of suffering as he did before the enemy, and to ask God to give him strength to bear his pain, and to grant him a speedy recovery. The poor fellow joyfully replied, "I have much more to be

" thankful for than to pray for." Another made
the remark to his minister, " The Saviour will have
" cripples. The people who are whole do not seek
" Him." There is much more true philosophy in
this than in the sentiment often uttered, that it is
better to be killed outright than to be maimed for
life. One officer boasted that he gave orders to the
soldiers to kill him in such an event, and that they
would find written authority for doing so in his
pocket, as he did not wish to live on earth as a
cripple! Some Austrian officers, too, shot themselves through the head with their own revolvers
rather than be taken prisoners; and this suicidal
act even found some who praised it as a deed of
valour!

One of the chaplains writes: " A superior officer
" who was severely wounded opened his heart to
" me more and more at each visit. We felt ourselves
" at one in the highest matters, and seemed as if we
" had known each other for a long time. I unex-
" pectedly introduced his wife to him, she having
" hastened hither from a distance. I knew that he

" had counselled her against taking the journey, and
" wished her to remain with the children. But
" when we were both alone he said to me with deep
" thankfulness, 'I have realised how God hears
" ' prayer. One night during last week I suffered
" ' much from being alone, and entreated the Lord
" ' right earnestly to send me a sympathising nurse.
" ' My wife has been telling me that she started off
" ' the next evening, urged hither by a feeling of
" ' unrest at being separated from me which she
" ' could not control.' "

Another reports : "I found a brother in the faith
" in the person of a young officer of eighteen years
" old. He was descended from the family of an old
" Count of the Empire in Hesse, and the traditions
" of his ancestry led him to enter the Austrian army.
" He had fallen badly wounded, and became a Prus-
" sian prisoner, but was attended with great care.
" At length his aunt, who was a Prussian subject, ar-
" rived; and shortly before his death his old gover-
" ness also. I confess that when he was alone I felt
" a particular drawing to his bedside, for I had not

" up to that time found such a childlike, pure, and
" believing heart amongst any of the soldiers, as he
" possessed. The veil of melancholy rested upon his
" finely-chiselled features, because he felt, even before
" I spoke to him, that God would call him away in
" the bloom of youth ; and now the seeds of a pious
" education were springing up amidst pains and
" sufferings. He made his confession with such
" fervour and humility that I was deeply affected ;
" and when he knew that he must die, he folded his
" hands and repeated the hymn of prayer, ' Christ, who
" ' is my life,' all through ; then his tears fell as he
" thought of his parents weeping for him. I can
" truly say, ' His soul pleased God. *Ave pia*
." ' *anima.*' "

There was a very general desire for the Lord's
Supper manifested, not only by those who saw the
near approach of death, but also by those who rejoiced in the signs of convalescence. It was affecting
to see the few Protestants amongst the Austrians
who could not speak German, making signs to the
chaplains to this effect. Many silent celebrations

have taken place by the couches of these men, the
sacred symbols supplying the place of words. On
one occasion a field preacher was administering the
Lord's Supper to a wounded Prussian, when a Magyar
lying in the same room attracted attention by saying,
" You." The chaplain went to him, but could not
understand a syllable that he said. When he was
on the point of going away to fetch an attendant,
the Magyar folded his hands imploringly, and added
the Sclavic words, " Pod sem" (come here). The
minister understood that it was he who was wanted,
and said the words, " Catholic? Calvinist?" The
sick man answered with the Magyar termination,
" Calvinist reformed," whereupon the question was
put to him by signs, "Do you desire the Lord's
Supper?" to which he answered affirmatively, and
received it with evident and hearty joy.

Pastor W—— relates a similar incident with a
Roumanian, who could only speak a few words of
German. " He had called repeatedly to the nursing
" sister, ' Priest, priest,' and she sent me to him.
" On my asking him if he were Protestant, he shook

" his head; that surprised me. I then called the
" Roman Catholic field chaplain, who was close by.
" He entered into conversation with the wounded
" man by words and signs, 'Are you Roman Ca-
" 'tholic?' The answer to this, as to all the other
" questions, was a continued shaking of the head.
" It was only when I held the chalice to him in an
" inquiring attitude that he stretched out his hands
" after it, and made me understand his wish. On
" receiving the sacrament, he whispered a prayer to
" me that was unintelligible; and after the service
" was over he looked bright and contented, and
" shook my hand in acknowledgment of his thanks."

Sometimes the chaplains were able to avail themselves of some one who understood both Hungarian
and German, who acted as interpreter on the occasion; and it once happened that a Jew discharged
the office of interpreter at the celebration of the
Lord's Supper, who seemed to be much impressed
with the service.

It must not be supposed, however, from the scenes
described above, that the experiences of the chaplains,

in their conversations with the wounded, were all of a pleasurable kind, though they had so much to encourage them. ↳ A Viennese Protestant retorted, when the minister spoke of heaven as a place where there was no pain, " No one knows that, because " no one has ever come back from thence." Very many of course showed themselves altogether indifferent and careless, and even impatient of religious conversation, while others listened quietly to the words of the minister; but the monotonous, " Yes, " yes," which was the only answer they gave, disclosed an inward, " no," or made it very difficult to approach them more closely. Some declined religious conversation altogether, on the pretence that it excited them too much; and one chaplain mentions that a man returned a book which he had given him, because it was too serious. One sick man declared that all religious intercourse, belief in God, prayer, sin, penitence, grace, were, in his opinion, only " views;" and on the chaplain asking him whether he belonged to the Freethinkers, he replied, " I " belong to no religion;" a remark which gave great offence to his comrades, who regarded it as a personal offence to their minister.

In the cholera hospitals, the chaplains sometimes experienced a difficulty of an altogether different character. Their approach to the bedside of a patient was often interpreted as a sign of his being very ill; and they were obliged to be especially cautious in administering the Lord's Supper, because many regarded it as tantamount to a sentence of death upon the recipient.

They were, moreover, often obliged to defer more to the opinions of the surgeons than was exactly agreeable to them; not that as a general rule they did not work harmoniously together, but as the surgeon is of necessity the supreme officer in a hospital, they had sometimes to restrain their zeal in deference to his authority. Among so large a body of men as the medical staff, there would be sure to be some who cared little or nothing for religion, and who would look upon the primary duties of the chaplain with disfavour; but even such, while restricting the religious exercises as much as

o

possible, could not but accept with thankfulness the assistance which the ministers rendered them in a hundred different ways, cheering the invalids by little acts of kindness, and relieving their minds by attending to any personal matters which might cause them anxiety; for all which the surgeon could not spare the time. Many of them, however, regarded the labours of the chaplains as of the highest importance, even from a medical point of view, holding the doctrine that a right and wholesome influence upon the mind and spirit of the sick, is conducive to physical well-being; and some of the surgeons in their reports have described, in strong terms, the benefits which they observed the men derived from such ministrations.

The clergy who were appointed to hospital duty received most valuable assistance from the deacons and deaconesses, as well as from the numerous voluntary sick nurses, male and female, of both confessions. In the hospitals of Northern Bohemia a deacon was attached to each minister, who assisted him in discharging his duties in the branch hospitals belonging to the larger establishments; and many of them were of sufficient experience to occupy the place of the chaplain when he was absent at some distant hospital.

They also acknowledge with gratitude the strict impartiality of the sisters of Roman Catholic orders, who respected the special wishes and needs of the Protestants, and used to read at their bedside out of the Protestant Prayer-books and devotional works with which the invalids had been supplied. Indeed, throughout the whole war, there was scarcely a single district in which the Christian love of both confessions did not unite harmoniously in works of ministry and Christian mercy.

The Knights of St. John have already been mentioned in these pages, though the great assistance rendered by them is very inadequately described. This order took charge of such ministers as arrived late in the field, and introduced them to those places where the need of spiritual attendance was especially urgent, indicating to them the ways and means of their further progress, which were often difficult to learn, and sustaining them with good counsel and vigorous action in every emergency. Moreover, the stores of the St. John's depôts supplied the hospital preachers with books and other necessaries, which substantially aided them in their labours amongst the sick; and the officers of the order often personally superintended the dispensing of bodily relief. Pastor Rogge gratefully acknowledges their services in the following words: " No hospital chaplain re-" turned home from this war without having had " cause to record, from personal experience, the good -" deeds of these knights of mercy, who combined " piety, the fear of God, and the power of faith and " love, with the courage, boldness, and faithful-" ness of their brothers and sons in the army, for " which the nobility of the German nation is so " distinguished. To them, as well as to all those " who have gone through this hard but invaluable " work on behalf of our wounded and sick brethren, " may the word of blessing be fulfilled, ' Inasmuch " ' as ye did it to one of the least of these My " ' brethren, ye have done it unto Me.' "

CHAPTER X.

BURIAL SERVICES.

THERE is but one other part of the chaplain's duties which remains to be described—that of committing the dead to their last resting-place. It occupied no inconsiderable portion of their valuable time, and often had to be done in a most hurried and unsatisfactory manner, though whenever possible the full service prescribed by the military regulations was celebrated.

The difficulty of carrying this out will be readily appreciated when the extent of the battle-ground and the rapidity of the army's movements are taken into consideration. For instance, it often happened that the troops took up their position at the close of an engagement, some three or four miles from the spot where it began, and where the men who fell first would still be lying. On such occasions it was neither possible to gather all the fallen together for a general funeral, nor to hold a separate service at each of the widely-scattered graves. All that could be done in such a case was to send back a detachment of troops with a commission to search for the fallen, and to gather them together in tens or twenties or more, and then (with the help of the country people, who often had to be pressed into the service) to dig a grave and bury their friends and foes without distinction in one common pile. Unless they happened to be a very rough lot who were told off to perform this last service to their comrades, they never omitted some sort of service, if only a silent Lord's Prayer, before going forward to another spot. Even this much could not always be accomplished, for in this war it sometimes happened that immediately on their having rested themselves after a battle they had to pursue their onward march, leaving the care of their dead to the division that might be in the rear.

On the 4th of July, the day after the battle of Königgrätz, there were graves dug at more than one hundred different spots on the broad field, in order to receive the bodies of the slain, whole battalions being employed as grave-diggers. The chaplains who were there were occupied all day, and to the utmost of their strength, with the wounded, so that it was simply impossible to pay the respect they would have wished to the dead: the utmost they could do was to offer up a short prayer and pronounce the benediction over those graves which were lying immediately in their way, even though they may have been already filled in.

The funeral solemnities were always duly attended to when they could be held in the presence of the battalion or regiment in whose ranks the dead men had fought; and there was no better opportunity of speaking to the hearts of the living than when they stood around the graves of their fallen comrades. The most reserved amongst them were at such moments open to serious words of warning, and to the truths of the Gospel. It was not uncommon on

such occasions to see the tears roll down the cheeks
of men who were thoroughly hardened—in most cases
perhaps tears of grief at the loss of a beloved friend
and comrade, or of a worthy commander, but sometimes, doubtless, tears of thankfulness at the remembrance of a wonderful personal deliverance. One
man remarked that the pieces of the same shell
which killed his neighbour had passed over his head
without hurting him, which surely read him a most
convincing lesson as to God's preserving and shel-
tering grace.

The form of burial service was generally short and
simple. If music were at hand, the band played a
verse of the chorale, "Jesus meine Zuversicht," which
was generally adopted by the Prussian army, or
" Was Gott thut, das ist wohlgethan;" then the chaplain, in his vestments, if possible, or in his simple
ministerial uniform, began : " In the name of God,
" the Father, Son, and Holy Ghost," and then threw
into the open grave the customary three handsfull of
earth, accompanied by the solemn words, " Dust thou
" art, and unto dust thou shalt return," as a last

salutation to the dead, and a serious warning to the living. Except in the hurried days of battle, this was followed by a short address, concluding with a prayer and the benediction. Many officers and soldiers have acknowledged that the impressions they received at these burial services were the most lasting of any; a testimony of no little worth, considering how quickly they were generally called away from such scenes to all the stir and excitement of the campaign.

The chaplain to the 1st division of Guards mentions having buried those who fell at the battle of Burgersdorf at the edge of a forest, which resounded all the time with the noise of the bivouac, for the troops had to cook their dinner in a hurry, so as to proceed on their march within an hour. Notwithstanding the busy hum, which almost drowned the minister's voice, a short but impressive service was held, the Fusileers (already formed into columns for the march) assembling at the graves of three of their young officers, Von der Mülbe, Von Sydow, and Von Byern, who had helped to purchase the new victory

of Soor on the previous day with their heart's blood.
The names of these sleeping men suggested rich
materials for a funeral address (which had, however,
to be limited to ten minutes), as the place itself was
sacred to the Prussian Guards as the scene of a
former victory, on which occasion also a Von Sydow
was amongst the slain. The two namesakes lie
buried near together. Their general, Von Hiller,
was deeply moved, and could not restrain his tears,
as he thanked the chaplain for his address, little
thinking, perhaps, that within a few days he would
be buried in like manner.

The scene just described took place on the 29th of
June ; that to which the closing passage refers took
place on the evening of the 4th of July upon the
heights of Chlum. The same chaplain thus describes
the scene :—" Here the commander of the 1st
" division of Foot Guards, General Von Hiller, was
" buried on the precise spot where he met his heroic
" death on the previous day. The place commanded
" a wide view over the extensive battle-field. Nine
" other graves were dug by the side of Hiller's, for

" the bodies of the superior officers of the division
" who had fallen. Unfortunately, in consequence of
" an order having been misunderstood, the greater
" portion of them were buried in the church of
" Chlum without any special service. First-Lieute-
" nant Von Helldorf was the only one who found his
" last resting-place by the side of Hiller. Imme-
" diately fronting the grave of the general were two
" very large pits, each of which contained from sixty
" to eighty bodies, principally of the men who had
" been swept off by the murderous struggle around
" the heights of Chlum. Not far from the graves a
" number of the cannon which had been captured
" were brought together. The king came to the
" funeral in order to honour, even in death, his fallen
" general, though his head-quarters were at two
" hours' distance, and the royal princes were also
" present. Besides the deputations from all the
" troops of the division, there were a large number
" who came of their own accord from the bivouac
" at Vsestar, in order to take part in the obsequies;
" and almost all the officers of the division were

" there. It was natural, therefore, that the service
" should bear reference not only to the graves which
" were lying open immediately before us, but to all
" those whom the brave general had led, and in
" whose midst he fell. I believe that I have never
" addressed a more solemn assembly, or one more
" stricken with grief, than the enormous gathering
" which stood that evening around the graves of the
" heroes of Chlum. David's funeral text: ' The
" ' beauty of Israel is slain upon thy high places.
" ' How are the mighty fallen !' furnished rich mate-
" rial for application to those who on the previous
" day had purchased glory on this very spot at the
" cost of their own lives. The place where we stood
" represented in all its proportions the greatness of
" the victory we had won, as well as the severity of
" the losses with which it was bought. Thankful-
" ness and joy must have struggled with the most
" painful grief, in the king's heart, at this moment.
" With evident emotion, he stepped forward to the
" edge of the graves at the close of the service, and
" rendered thanks as he cast in the handful of earth

" in honour of the fallen. On this occasion military
" honours were paid, though they had previously
" been discontinued by order, because the troops had
" not been supplied with blank cartridges. The
" whistling of the balls over the graves at the com-
" mand, ' Fire high,' produced a most peculiar im-
" pression : the brave ones had fallen on the pre-
" vious day to the sound of the same music. It was
" indeed a military farewell."

The churchyard of Chlum witnessed more funerals
on the following day. There, young Soosen, the
adjutant of the general was buried, who appears to
have fallen at the side of his superior in the same
shower of bullets, but whose body was not found in
time to be buried along with him. Colonel Von
Pape also buried his only son there, who succumbed
to his wounds after twenty-four hours' suffering; and
the chaplain mentions that as he was going there to
officiate at this last service, he passed a man who was
making a rude coffin for his son out of the remains
of an old fence.

When the active operations were over, the comrades of the fallen, and the members of the order of St. John, busily occupied themselves in identifying the burial-places as far as possible, and in marking them as Christian graves by the erection of a simple cross, on which they inscribed such details as they could gather. Thus on the first wooded height behind Sadowa stands one with the following inscription: "Here lie 4 officers and 68 men of the 4th " and 6th Pomeranian Regiments of Foot, and 1 " Austrian major;" the names of the four Prussian officers being added below. Before Chlum stands a cross with the simple inscription: "Here rest 55 " Austrians, 3rd July, 1866." Close by the village is a large pit, containing about four hundred bodies, and in the neighbourhood are also single graves with crosses and cyphers. The ground where Lieutenant-General Baron Hiller and the First-Lieutenant Von Helldorf lie has been bought by the Order of St. John, who are going to set up a head-stone. Behind Chlum, looking towards Königgrätz, stands a cross with this inscription: "Here rest 7 " Austrian officers, 9 grenadiers of the Second Prus-

" sian Regiment of Guards, and 1 artilleryman ;"
and right opposite to this is another, on which has
been burnt with a hot iron, " Royal Prussian Lieu-
" tenant Von Maltzahn, 9th company of the Regiment
" of Fusileer Guards." Below the mountain of Ross-
beritz is an inscription to this effect : " Here rest in
" God, 2 grenadiers of the 4th and 9th companies of
" the 1st Regiment of Foot Guards ;" while an
adjoining grave indicates the resting-place of two
Prussians and thirty-nine Austrians. It is needless,
however, to multiply details. These will serve as a
specimen of the sad memorials which mark the track
of the victorious army.

The chaplains found it more difficult to administer
consolation at the graves of those who were snatched
away by the pestilence that walketh in darkness,
than of those who fell in battle. As a matter of
expediency, however, their duties in this respect were
soon reduced to a minimum, as the military authorities ordered that during the height of the cholera
the bodies should be buried silently under cover of
the night, in order not to increase the alarm. The

service was then limited to a short prayer and the benediction; but in some places, such as Lundenburg, this had to be repeated three times a day. Pastor Trogisch writes: " That was always the most " difficult part of my office. I shall never forget " the place selected on this side of the Taya, near to " the edge of a forest, where two hundred to three " hundred of our brave Prussians found their resting- " place in large common graves. The earth is " indeed consecrated, for many prayers have risen " up from that spot to the Lord; but I never looked " at it without a shudder, as it recalled the scenes I " had witnessed. The Slowacks used to drive their " one-horse carts filled with dead bodies; they took " off the coverings from the half-naked corpses, dis- " torted by struggle and death, and laid them by " tens in the large grave. All flesh is grass! The " red uniform, which a short time before covered fresh " young fellows, contrasted horribly with their ghastly " forms wasted by disease. May they be at peace ! " May the Lord have received their souls into His pre- " sence ! Many sighs after home lie buried there."

The numerous graves in Brünn bear a silent but impressive witness to the presence of the victorious Prussian army in the summer of 1866, as well as to the devastation which the cholera wrought in its ranks. For a long time past the Christians of both confessions have buried their dead in the cemetery belonging to the town, not in separate quarters, but mingled together in well-defined groups. Whole rows may now be seen bearing Prussian names. There a cross bearing the name of some officer, again a pile of stones erected to the memory of another, be he Prussian or Austrian; then another encircled with a laurel wreath, erected to the memory of Lieutenant von Froreich, bearing the motto " The earth is the " Lord's," which was the answer of his afflicted mother when it was proposed to her to carry the body of her son home for burial. Close by are the memorials of Frederick Krüger, a deacon, and of Dr. Zueger, an assistant surgeon, both of whom were smitten with the cholera while attending to the duties of their office; and then a simple wooden cross indicates the last resting-place of a poor sutler whose

P

name remains unknown. By far the largest portion of the Prussians who died at Brünn were, however, buried in the cemetery of Obrowitz. There are two large pits, in which 1385 men of that army await the resurrection day. The bodies of the Prussians were carried in a train of waggons every evening from the various hospitals, and brought to this place for burial. It was a sad sight to watch the carts go round in the dusk, from the Blind Asylum to the Gymnasium, and thence to the Polytechnic School, the Spielberg, and so on, until at last they reached the cemetery. The coffins were black, with long white crosses upon them, and they used to be placed in the pit side by side in a row, and covered over with a layer of earth, the process being repeated nightly until the grave was filled to within about five feet of the surface. One day, however, there were no coffins to be had, as the joiners of Brünn were unable to supply the large number required. A mound has been thrown up upon the spot, and a plain cross of polished granite erected within a little flower-garden, for the proper maintenance of which the general in command has placed a small fund in the hands of the Protestant church at Brünn. A special service was held at the consecration of this memorial on the 28th August, at which the whole garrison was present. After singing the chorale, " Jesus meine Zuversicht," the words of consecration were uttered by the Protestant and Roman Catholic chaplains in the name of their respective churches, followed by a prayer, after which the salvoes of a battalion which was posted by the wall of the cemetery proclaimed, as with the sound of three thunderclaps, the conclusion of a ceremony in which the townspeople as well as the soldiery took equal interest.

A service of a similar nature was held on the occasion of the erection of a large cross by Count Theodore von Stolberg in the graveyard of Lundenburg; another at Königinhof, where a new burial-ground was established by the side of the old cemetery, and in which about four hundred lie buried, most of whom perished from their wounds.

These special services furnished the chaplains with excellent opportunities of bringing the word of God

before their people, and they formed a good substi-
tute for the public services, which circumstances
compelled them sometimes to omit for a long time
together; while they also enabled them to show forth
their Protestant faith before those in whose midst
they left their dead. The townspeople always took
part in the funerals; and though doubtless often
attracted by curiosity, they usually followed the service with the closest attention, the very simplicity of
which evidently made a great impression upon them,
at least for the moment. Surely the good seed of
the Gospel cannot always have fallen on unfruitful
soil. Perhaps many graves in these foreign lands
will not only tell of the Prussians buried there, but
of the Gospel which was also made known there as
the power of God unto salvation.

It was very rarely that ignorance or religious pre-
judice showed themselves in respect to the burial of
the dead : only one or two such instances are worth
recording. At one place the Romish priest did not
wish to allow a jaeger of the Guards to be buried in
his cemetery, and suggested a spot separated by a

wall from the churchyard, and which was devoted to
those who committed suicide and to heretics. The
commander of the battalion hesitated about demand-
ing a proper grave, fearing that the body would be
exhumed after the departure of the troops, and contented himself with having the dividing wall removed.
There they buried their dead, comforting themselves,
like the mother recently mentioned, with the belief
that all "the earth is the Lord's." The chaplain
did not refrain from telling the inhabitants of the
place that this stranger (who had specially distinguished himself in battle, and who bore the character
of a pious and God-fearing youth) had found just as
honourable a grave as any one who was lying in the
adjoining cemetery, and begged them to hold as
sacred the duty of Christian hospitality, even to the
dead.

A curious case occurred at Kremsier, the residence
of the Archbishop of Olmütz. It is the custom of
the country to bury the dead with their faces turned
towards the east, in readiness for the morning of the
resurrection; but it was observed that the grave-

digger was in the habit of burying his co-religionists
on the one side, and the Protestants on the other,
turning the latter towards the west.   On being asked
by one of the chaplains why he did not bury them
together, and why he turned the Protestants in the
opposite direction, his answer was, "I am instructed
" to bury the Christians here, and the others there."
The military authorities taught him and his superiors that they were all Christians, and insisted that
they should be all buried together, without distinction of confession.

Such instances were happily quite the exception.
More edifying is the account of a united funeral
which the Protestant chaplain describes in the following words: " We walked before the bier, the
" Roman Catholic priest in his rich vestments, I in
" my field-gown and bands, but he quite understood
" that 'it is not the cowl that makes the monk.'
" The priest offered up his 'De Profundis,' I conse-
" crated my dead, offered up an extempore prayer,
" and repeated the confession of our most holy faith,
" concluding with the Lord's Prayer.   He then re-

" peated his Paternoster, and taking up the shovel,
" cast some earth upon the grave, after which he
" handed it to me, and I did the same. How goodly
" such brotherly union is, in contrast with that sepa-
" ration which even the grave does not prevent!
" We experienced there the truth of the apostolic
" words, ' We are all one in Christ Jesus.' "

After the war was over, endeavours were made to
identify, as far as possible, the graves of those who
were left behind, and funds were raised to supply
them with crosses of wood or iron, upon which such
information as could be obtained has been inscribed.
The whole line of route from the Saxon frontiers to
the very gates of Vienna is now full of mournful
interest to hundreds of German families, and some
spots claim the affection of a still wider circle. Many
of the engagements took place in the neighbourhood
of battle-fields well known in history, and the records
in the graveyards become still more interesting by
reason of the varied associations they suggest. The
Prussians committed 136 of their number to the
grave in the military cemetery of Paasdorf, a village

situated not far from the celebrated field of Austerlitz. A large iron cross indicates their resting-place in the graveyard which was specially assigned to the military at the time of the French invasions in 1805 and 1809. The heroes of Königgrätz and Sadowa lie there beside the victors of Austerlitz. Warriors of various nations, French, Austrians, and Russians, more recently Italians and Danes, who died in military captivity, and last of all the Prussians, have found their long home within this enclosure, and after their earthly struggles rest peaceably together, awaiting the grand summons which shall gather them together in one army under the banners of one King.

LONDON: PRINTED BY W. CLOWES AND SONS, STAMFORD STREET AND CHARING CROSS.